THE GREAT EASTERN SINCE 1900

CHARLES PHILLIPS

LONDON

IAN ALLAN LTD

First published 1985

ISBN 0 7110 1402 7

Published by Ian Allan Ltd, Shepperton, Surrey;
and printed by Ian Allan Printing Ltd at their works
at Coombelands in Runnymede, England

It has been a conscious decision to include in this volume
photographs of historic interest which might in other
circumstances have been excluded on grounds of quality.
It is hoped that the reader will accept the consequent
reduction in the production quality of some plates.

Photographs from the Locomotive & General Railway
Photographs collection are reproduced courtesy of David
& Charles Ltd.

Illustrations credited to the LCGB are from the Ken Nunn
collection, reproduced courtesy of the Locomotive Club
of Great Britain.

Cover painting by George F. Heiron

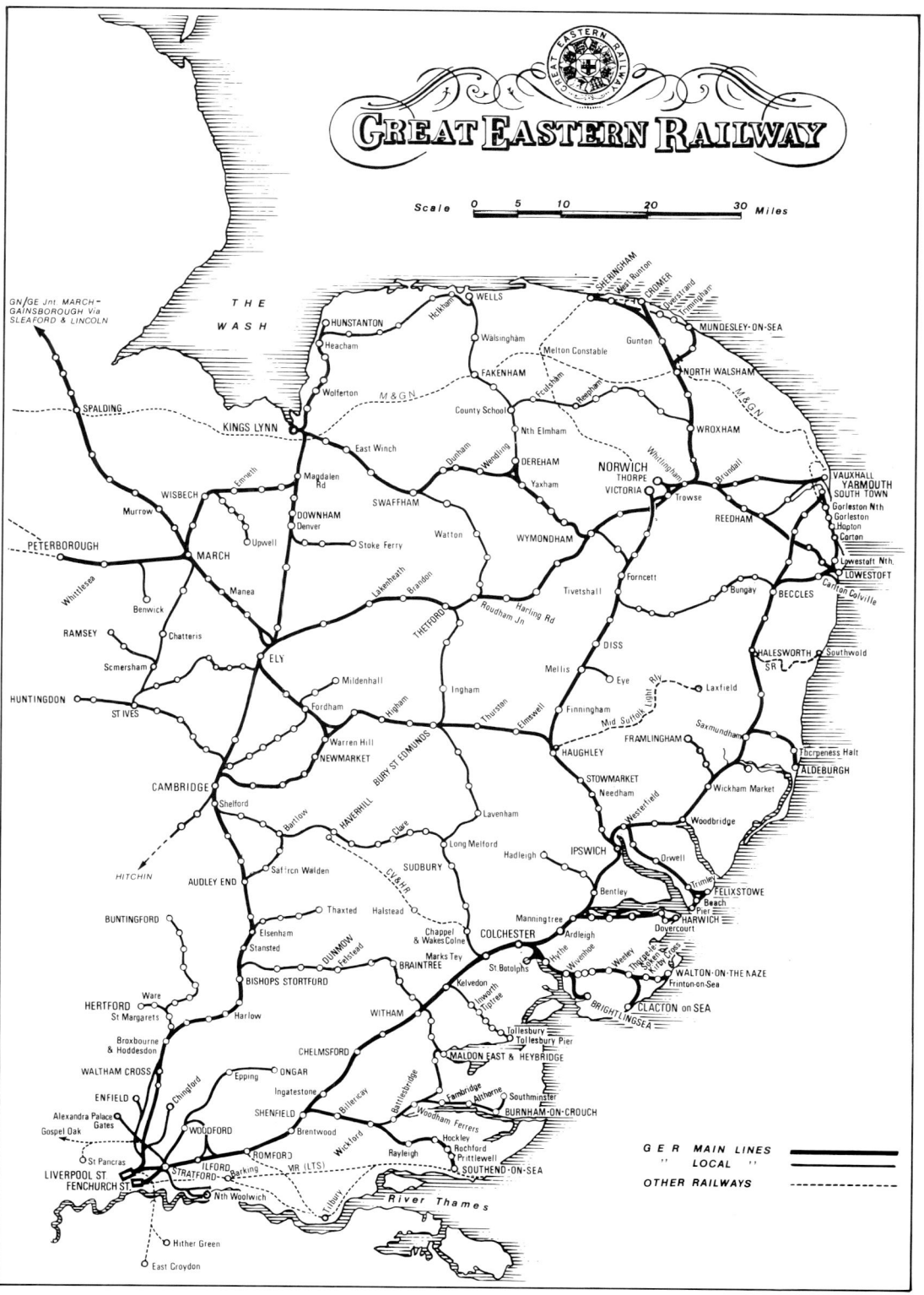

Introduction

History
1839-1900

The Great Eastern Railway had begun life on 7 August 1862 as the result of the amalgamation of the Eastern Counties, Norfolk, East Anglian, Newmarket and Eastern Union Railways. Of these companies the oldest was the Eastern Counties which had opened its first section of line, from Mile End to Romford on 18 June 1839. This was part of a proposed line from London to Yarmouth via Colchester, Ipswich and Norwich. By 29 March 1843 the line had reached Colchester, having cost nearly double what had been authorised originally for the entire line to Norwich! At Colchester the line stopped as Parliament would not allow it to go any further. Part of the difficulty was due to fact that the line was built on a gauge of 5ft. In 1844 this was altered to 4ft 8½in. On 1 January of the same year the Eastern Counties took a lease of the Northern & Eastern Railway which joined it at Stratford and by that date had reached Bishops Stortford; there was also a branch to Hertford. On 29 July 1845 the Northern & Eastern Railway extended its line from Bishops Stortford to Newport (Essex) on the same as the Eastern Counties, having now decided to reach Yarmouth via Cambridge, Ely and Norwich, opened its line from Newport to Brandon (Norfolk). There it connected with the Norfolk Railway's line to Yarmouth via Norwich.

The first section of the Norfolk Railway had been opened on 1 May 1844 from Norwich to Yarmouth. The extension to Brandon was opened on 29 July 1845. On 8 May 1848 the Eastern Counties took a lease of the Norfolk Railway. In the meantime the people of Ipswich felt a little bit left out in the cold and so they promoted the Eastern Union Railway which was opened from Colchester to Ipswich on 11 June 1846. On 24 December of that year the Ipswich & Bury Railway extended the line to Bury St Edmunds. The two railways amalgamated on 9 July 1847. Meanwhile construction started on building a line from Haughley to Norwich which was completed on 7 November 1849. The two main lines to Norwich were now complete. Of these the northern one served more centres of population, and a line from Chelmsford to Bury St Edmunds following the route used by stage coaches which might have provided the basis for another route, was never started. Other lines built during the period from 1840 were the Newmarket Railway from Great Chesterford opened on 3 January 1848 and the Ely to

Peterborough line of the Eastern Counties Railway on 14 January 1847. In 1846 and 1847 the East Anglian Railway built the line from Ely to King's Lynn, and in 1848 the March-Wisbech line. The 1850s saw the Newmarket Railway open its line from Cambridge to Six Mile Bottom on 9 October 1851 and close the line from the latter place to Great Chesterford on the same day, whilst on 1 June 1859 the East Suffolk Railway was completed from Ipswich to Lowestoft and was promptly taken over by the Eastern Counties Railway. Harwich had been reached from Manningtree on 15 August 1854.

By 1880 the Eastern Counties Railway had acquired the working of all the major railways in the Eastern Counties, but it was 1862 before they were incorporated into the Great Eastern Railway, except for the Northern & Eastern Railway which was not finally acquired until 1902.

The early years of the Great Eastern Railway were marked by financial difficulties and at one period it was actually insolvent. It was also during this time that the Marquis of Salisbury became Chairman. In 1900 he was the Prime Minister.

The 1870s saw the opening of Liverpool Street station on 2 February 1874 and the building of a number of lines in northeast London; whilst in 1879 following nearly thirty years war with each other or constiuents, the Great Eastern and the Great Northern formed a joint committee to operate and construct lines from Huntingdon to Doncaster via March, Spalding and Lincoln. The line came into operation in 1882 the same year that the Clacton branch was opened. Five years earlier (1877) had seen Cromer and Felixstowe reached by rail. The latter by an independent company which was taken over by the GER in 1885. In 1889 the Railway reached Southend. The 1890s saw the completion on 2 April 1894 of the East side of Liverpool Street station and the formation of the Norfolk & Suffolk Joint Committee with the Midland & Great Northern Joint Railway. The latter was the GER's main rival in Norfolk and had been built in stages by independent companies between 1877 and 1887 and was taken over by the two larger companies in its title in 1893. The first result of the new co-operation was the opening of the Mundesley branch on 1 July 1898.

The
Great Eastern

— An
Appreciation

Why 1900 as the starting date for this book? Why not say 1862 or 1923 or 1948? What is so particular about 1900?

The reason that I chose 1900 as the starting date is to some extent a personal one. If one were to make a list of particular years associated with the various railway companies of the British Isles for the period 1830 to 1948 one would undoubtably find that the Great Eastern fitted into the year 1900. One associates that year with the Great Eastern. It was the new year that engine No 1900 *Claud Hamilton* appeared and was exhibited at the Paris International Exhibition, winning a Gold Medal in the process. People associate railways with engines and the 'Claud Hamiltons' with their side-windowed cabs, leading bogies, copper capped chimneys and coupling rod splashers represented to both the people of the day and later generations a new epoch on the Great Eastern. Even the company thought it was a new epoch; why else was *Claud Hamilton* numbered 1900 when the highest previous number in the company's list was 1119?

There is another reason. 1900 was the year when the photography of trains in motion had reached a stage where it was becoming common. 1900 photographs of moving trains are not very common and before 1890 very rare. No, the 1900s were the first decade when people started to take photographs of trains in motion, so what is more logical than to start at 1900?

By 1900 most of the Great Eastern's network was complete. There only remained three new lines to be opened independently, plus two more jointly with the Midland & Great Northern Joint Committee. The Great Eastern was firmly established as the railway of the Eastern counties. Let us now examine its progress from that date.

In 1900 the Great Eastern's coaching stock consisted mainly of four- and six-wheeled carriages together with a few bogie carriages. The goods stock was almost entirely composed of unbraked four-wheel wagons. The locomotive stock was dominated by three types: the 2-4-0 for passenger trains except those on the suburban lines, the 0-6-0 for goods trains excepting shunting duties and the 0-6-0T for both suburban trains and shunting work. There were also 2-4-2T and 0-4-4T locomotives which worked both suburban and branch line trains, 0-4-0Ts which performed some shunting duties and worked the Wisbech & Upwell Tramway, 0-4-2Ts which

Above:
At the beginning of 1900, the Great Eastern's top rank express locomotives were the 10 Class P43 4-2-2s built in 1898. Although these were credited to James Holden, they were in fact the work of the Chief Locomotive Designer — Frederick Russell. Russel designed the GER's locomotives until about 1912. No 19 is seen here on an up Cromer express near Shenfield in 1900. The three clerestory roofed coaches are the self-contained restaurant car set.
L&GRP (21169)

helped work branch line passenger trains; 4-4-0s which shared main line trains with the 2-4-0s and 2-2-2s, and 4-2-2s which hauled the crack expresses of the day. The oldest and some of the best engines were the Johnson 'Little Sharpie' 2-4-0s originally built at the end of the 1860s. With a few exceptions all engines had inside cylinders.

During the period 1900-1922, the Great Eastern train continued to evolve, albeit very slowly, but fairly noticeably. In 1900 all engines had round-topped fireboxes and on 17 March that year there emerged from Stratford works 4-4-0 locomotive No 1900 *Claud Hamilton* (after the railway's chairman) the first of the famous class and the first Great Eastern engine to be fitted with the famous side windowed cab. As mentioned elsewhere, this engine was exhibited at the Paris Exhibition of that year, and along with a number of Great Eastern express engines of the day was equipped to burn oil fuel instead of coal. In 1900 there also appeared a 0-6-0 version of the 'Claud Hamiltons'. In 1902 came the first Belpaire fireboxed engine, No 1189 — an 0-6-0. Bogie carriages became more and more commonplace, and in 1904 the first corridor train sets appeared on the 'Hook Continental'. Later on, other trains received corridor sets including the famous 'Norfolk Coast Express', which with the 'Hook Continental' and the 'North Country Continental' were the pride of the Great Eastern. Vacuum-braked goods wagons began to appear and the engines working trains composed of these vehicles were of course fitted with the vacuum brake.

Side-windowed versions of the famous 'Gobbler' 2-4-2Ts of 1884 and the 'Buckjumper' 0-6-0T of 1886 were produced; but not of the legendary 'Little Goods' — the 'Y14' (later 'J15') 0-6-0s of 1883. Engines of the latter class continued to be built until 1913, when they totalled 289 locomotives.

There were occasional diversions of which the most famous was the 'Decapod' 0-10-0T of 1902. It has been claimed that this was the only locomotive built to defeat a parliamentary bill — in this case a bill promoting a tube railway. The engine succeeded. but was too heavy for the Great Eastern's bridges and was rebuilt into the company's only 0-8-0 and was finally scrapped in 1913. There were quite a number of abortive designs including three in 1903 for a railmotor for the Felixstowe-Felixstowe Pier branch and one in 1912 for a 4-6-2T. The Great Eastern was very much a small engine railway; the only exception to this being the '1500' class 4-6-0s of 1911.

Between 1900 and 1914 the Great Eastern had got rid of a large number of engines of

Above.
In the same year as the previous photograph, 'Claud Hamilton' 4-4-0 No 1891 hurtles through Brentwood station with an up express. This engine and No 19 are both oil burners, which accounts for the small hole just below the smokebox door. This admitted air, which was heated by coils in the smokebox and then injected together with oil fuel into the firebox. *L&GRP (21165)*

diverse classes dating back to the 1860s and 1870s. In 1914 there were a number of locomotives which would still be in service when steam finished at Stratford in 1962.

In 1900 there were few trains offering refreshment facilities, but by 1914 these were available on a reasonable number of trains on the main line as well as some on the outer suburban service to Southend.

In 1912, the London, Tilbury and Southend Railway, the Great Eastern's rival in south Essex, shook the GE by selling itself to the Midland Railway. The GE retaliated by barring the LT&S's 4-6-4Ts then under construction from entering Fenchurch Street station over the section of GER from Gas Factory Junction. During the period 1900 to 1914, three new lines were opened by the GER. These were: the Fairlop loop in 1903, the Tollesbury branch in 1904 and the Thaxted branch in 1913. Meanwhile as a partner in the Norfolk & Suffolk Joint Committee with the Midland & Great Northern Joint Railway, it opened lines from Yarmouth to Lowestoft in 1903 and Mundesley to Runton West Junction in 1906. In 1909 the Churchbury loop, opened in 1891, was closed to passenger traffic. On 4 August 1914, World War 1 broke out, during which the Great Eastern had rather a hectic time. Besides helping to supply the Fleet at Harwich and the 44 military camps set up in addition to locations where troops were already stationed, it undertook a certain amount of work for the Ministry of Munitions, constructed a couple of ambulance trains and sent 45 Class Y14 0-6-0s over to

France, where they worked nearer to the Front than any other British locomotives. The company also introduced the Radical Alterations timetable in October 1914 and towards the end of the war ran a farm in Suffolk as part of its policy of promoting agriculture. During the war two services were started specifically for munitions workers. The first one was in 1915 on the Churchbury Loop and was withdrawn in 1919. The other service was between Ilford and North Woolwich via Statford East Curve and ceased in 1921. This was the only passenger service to use the Stratford East Curve. The greatest visual impact of the war on the Great Eastern was the replacement of the rich royal blue livery by a rather drab grey one; consequently only one of the 'L77' ('N7') 0-6-2Ts which first entered service in 1915 was ever painted blue. The 'L77s' were the GERs most powerful suburban tank engine but because of the war only two (Nos 1000 and 1001) were built before 1921 and only 12 were in service by the grouping.

In 1920 the Great Eastern introduced Pullman Cars on a number of services including that to

Southend. Initially only first class cars were provided, but later third class cars were added as well. The Pullman Cars were not very successful as it was necessary to pay a supplement to ride in one, which East Anglians did not like, but the all-Pullman train the 'Eastern Belle' of a few years later was most successful. 1920 also saw the inauguration of the famous 'Jazz' service on the Chingford, Enfield and Palace Gates lines. This was the most intensive suburban service in the world operated by steam traction and offered a greater frequency of trains than anywhere else at that time. The year also saw the introduction of the 'D81' (later 'J20') 0-6-0s which until 1942 were the most powerful machines of their wheel arrangement in the country. At this time the GER borrowed from the Government some Great Central-type 2-8-0s which were used on the Great Eastern and Great Northern Joint line. In 1920 the Company wanted to buy 20 or 30 of the South Eastern & Chatham-type 2-6-0s which were being built by the Government at Woolwich Arsenal, but because delivery of the engines by 30 September could not be guaranteed the request was declined by the Government.

In August 1921 the Railways Act was passed and this signified the end of the Great Eastern Railway. Under the Act the Railway was to become part of the group which became the London & North Eastern Railway. This came into effect on 1 January 1923.

Let us now see what position the Great Eastern was in on 31 December 1922. For a start, bogie carriages were the norm on main-line trains, although six-wheelers were occasionally to be found. On suburban lines also, bogie carriages were becoming frequent, although six- and four-wheelers could also be found. Corridor trains offering refreshment facilities were usual on the crack expresses and some of the less important trains. There were, of course, the Pullman Cars as well. Turning now to goods trains; compared with 1900 there were a large number of vacuum-braked goods wagons, although these were only used on express goods trains which were quite often hauled by express passenger engines. Turning to the engines themselves; compared to 1900 there was less dominance by any particular wheel arrangement. Even 0-6-0s did not have the goods side to themselves. The 'Y14' 0-6-0s were the dominant class on the railway with 272 engines, but they

did not rule the roost. Not for that matter did the 'Claud Hamiltons'. The railway had not gone in for any experimental signalling installations during the period 1900-1922, but electric lighting was being installed in its carriages. Any major developments of a technical nature would have to be left to the London & North Eastern Railway.

Under the London & North Eastern Railway the Great Eastern section came to include not only the GER but also the Colne Valley and Halstead Railway and the Mid Suffolk Light Railway.

One of the first things that the new company did was to introduce a rather pleasant apple green livery to the 'Claud Hamiltons' and the '1500s'. It also continued the construction of the latter class and the 'N7s'. Engines from other sections began to appear. The first, in 1923, were some Great Northern 'K2' 2-6-0s. The LNER's main concern was the lack of heavy goods engines on the GER. Firstly it sent some Great Central 'O4' 2-8-0s and Hull & Barnsley 'Q10' 0-8-0s; and then in 1932 it built a batch of 'O2' 2-8-0s specifically for the GE section.

On the passenger side the LNER provided new main-line carriages, secondary line carriages and suburban line carriages, the last being the well-known articulated 'Quint art' sets, so called because each set consisted of five coaches. Express passenger motive power was strengthened in 1928 by the introduction of the famous Class B17 'Sandringham' 4-6-0s, whilst the early 1930s saw the rebuilding of several Great Eastern types such as the 'Claud Hamiltons' and the 'B12s'. During the 1930s, services were accelerated to enable these engines to be used to their best ability over what were, and still are, the most difficult main lines out of London. By the summer of 1939, the Class B17s and the rebuilt Class B12s enabled the Great Eastern section to provide a service which compares well with that offered in 1983, and was faster than present-day road coach services. In 1957 two members of Class B17, named *East Anglian* and *City of London* were streamlined for use on the 'East Anglian' express. Besides the 'B17s' only one other class was designed by the LNER specifically for the GE and this was a 2-6-4T for the Southend services in 1927, but for a number of reasons it never left the drawing board.

The early 1930s saw the rebuilding of several Great Eastern types such as the 'Claud

Hamiltons' and the 'B12s'. Other important classes of engine introduced in the inter-war period by the LNER were the 'J39' 0-6-0s in the late 1920s, the 'K3' 2-6-0s in 1938 and the 'V1' 2-6-2Ts in 1939. The 'J39s' were particularly useful and could handle almost any type of train. In addition, members of several pre-grouping classes were transferred from other sections of the LNER. One tragic feature of the inter-war period was the closure of several branch lines to passenger traffic. On a more hopeful note the LNER started work on electrifying the lines from Liverpool Street and Fenchurch Street to Shenfield, whilst London Transport began conversion of the lines from Leyton to Ongar and Newbury Park as part of the extension of the Central Line from Liverpool Street. The period also saw the widening of the Colchester line to Shenfield and the enlargement of Whitemoor yards at March. On 3 September 1939 World War 2 began. The impact of this was considerable on the GE. Besides once again having the Fleet at Harwich, there were initially various RAF and later United States airfields to be supplied, whilst the East End of London took the full impact of the Blitz in 1940 and 1941. The War Department took several 0-6-0Ts permanently and some 2-4-2Ts temporarily for use on armoured trains. The War Department in return loaned some British Army Austerity 2-8-0s and 2-10-0s and some American Army Class S160 2-8-0s. The war years also saw in 1943 the arrival of the 'B1' 4-6-0s and in 1944 the 'J45' 0-6-0 diesel shunters. These later were the first diesel locomotives to appear on the Great Eastern. In 1945 10 'B17s' were rebuilt with two cylinders into 'B2s'.

In 1945 the war ended. People travelling on those lines for which electrification was promised, and in particular residents of north Ilford, started making rumblings about what they considered to be the shortcomings of the steam services. The press and 10 Downing Street got hold of it and work restarted on the projects. On 5 May 1947 the first London Transport Central line electric trains reached Leytonstone and by 31 December had got out to Woodford. It should be pointed out that these electric trains were not newly built ones of the 1938-type stock as on the Northern and Bakerloo lines, but of the older standard stock going back to the mid-1920s which had been displaced from the other two tube lines. As they had been stored in the open in some instances since 1939, they tended to be unreliable in the early days. They were replaced with 1959/62 stock by the middle of 1963. By the end of 1947 orders had also been placed for the electric trains for the Shenfield line. On 1 January 1948, the Nationalisation of Britain's

railways took effect and British Railways was born. Let us have a look at the position of the Great Eastern on 31 December 1947.

The most important thing was that some part of the system had an electric train service, whilst work was in hand to provide it to other parts. Included in this was the Ilford Flyover which had been opened a few months previously. There were colour light signals on the Chingford and Southend lines and on the Colchester main line as far as Chelmsford. The LNER had provided hump marshalling yards at March, Temple Mills and Goodmayes. Goods wagons were goods wagons and consequently there was a mixture of braked and un-braked vehicles. In terms of passenger rolling stock, there were no four-wheel carriages left in service and only a few six-wheel ones which were to be found on the Thaxted & Elsenham, the Kelvedon & Tollesbury and the Mid Suffolk Light Railways. For the rest of the system all carriages were bogie ones. There were also a few gas-lit vehicles about. As for locomotives, there was a wonderful variety to be found. There were survivors from the Great Eastern including 'J15s' dating back to the 1880s and three crane tank engines at Stratford dating back to the 1860s. There were also 18 'E4' 2-4-0s which could give a Victorian aura to any passenger train that they hauled. There were locomotives from the Great Northern, Great Central and North Eastern Railways as well as ones built by the London & North Eastern Railway.

Within a few months of nationalisation, 'L1' 2-6-4Ts began appearing on the Great Eastern, whilst the next year (1949) saw the arrival of the 'K1' 2-6-0s. Had nationalisation not taken place,

the LNER's proposed lightweight 2-6-0s (the 'K6' class) would have been built and in all probability have run over the GER lines. For that matter, diesel multiple-units might have reached the line earlier.

Although not figuring in the routes used in the 1948 locomotive exchanges the Great Eastern did see in the spring of that year the test of a Southern Railway 'Battle of Britain' class 4-6-2. For the summer timetables of 1950 and 1951 further examples were loaned to Stratford.

Meanwhile electrification continued to advance. In the spring of 1948 the London Transport Central Line reached Loughton plus the Chigwell loop and in September of the following year, Epping. London Transport then took over the Ongar branch which had to wait until November 1957 for electric trains. September 1949 also saw the first British Railways electric trains using 1,500V dc start running between Liverpool Street and Shenfield.

1950 saw the start of the Clacton Interval Service operated by 'B1s' and 'B2s'. In 1951 came the first 'Britannia' 4-6-2s which, aided by brilliant scheduling of first the Norwich and then several years later the Clacton Interval services, managed to create a revolution on the GE. The 'Britannias' were well liked and when late in 1951 two Standard '5' 4-6-0s were loaned they did not sparkle; the same thing happened in 1959 with a 'Clan' 4-6-2. On a more sour note the early 1950s saw the beginning of a round of branch line closures. A possible saviour of branch lines appeared in 1953 when the ACV experimental diesel railcar was tried out on the Ongar and Southminster branches.

In 1954 British Railways introduced their last

steam type — the '9F' 2-10-0s and some of these were used between Whitemoor Yard (March) and Temple Mills Yard (Stratford). In the same year BR announced its Modernisation Plan. If one of the ideas on electrification had been realised there would not have been much of the GE that would not have been electrified.

In 1955 came the first fruits of the Modernisation Plan — the first production diesel multiple-unit. The next year saw the first electric trains reach Chelmsford and Southend, whilst the first main-line diesels (the Brush Type 2) arrived in 1957, followed in 1958 by the English Electric Type 4s. The beginning of 1958 had the GE still operating an enormous variety of different steam engines. It was the only line to have both 2-4-0s (the 'E4s') and 2-10-0s, but there now began a ruthless attack on steam. A few engines were preserved including the last 'E4', but two notable classes — the 'D16' 4-4-0s (better known as the 'Claud Hamiltons') and the 'F5' 2-4-2Ts — were scrapped in their entirety. As replicas are now starting to be made of various unpreserved classes, perhaps someone could do the same for these — and a 'Y6' 0-4-0 tram locomotive, also possibly a 'Little Sharpie' and a 'B17' 'Sandringham'.

The year 1959 saw electric trains start running from Colchester to Clacton and Walton using high voltage alternating current. These trains were what are now Class 302 electric multiple-units. In November 1960 the northeast London suburban services were electrified using AC current. Included in this scheme was the Churchbury Loop which was now re-opened to passengers, having been previously closed to them in 1919. The direct current suburban electric lines to Chelmsford and Southend were converted to AC at the same time. The Lea Valley line was not electrified until 1969 and until then had Liverpool Street's only diesel suburban service. The North Woolwich service which did not run into Liverpool Street remained steam worked, and had the distinction of being London's last scheduled steam suburban service. In the spring of 1962 electric working first became possible between London and Clacton. Until the electric trains designed for the service were ready, most trains were diesel-hauled although a few electrics were run (including most of the Sunday service and the weekday service to Witham) using suburban electric units. During the summer of that year, the electric units for the

service had their first trials on the GE and in the January of the following year they went into regular service.

On 9 September 1962 the last steam trains arrived and left Liverpool Street station bringing to a close main line steam on the Great Eastern. The previous day had seen the last steam suburban train on the Palace Gates to North Woolwich service. In November of the following year March shed shut its doors to steam and so ended the steam era on the GE. (The last steam engines of all were a couple of 'Y3' 0-4-0 Sentinel shunters which lingered on at Lowestoft sleeper depot until 1966). 1963 also saw the publication of the Beeching Report which spell or threatened to spell the end of many branch and secondary lines and goods yards. The position of the GER on 31 December 1963 was that it was for all practical purposes steamless. All trains were either formed of diesel or electric multiple-units or were hauled by diesel-electrical locomotives. Locomotives were not very old. The oldest were some London North Eastern Railway diesel shunters of 1944 at March. The oldest main-line engine was Brush Type 2 No D5500 dating from 1957. Diesel multiple-units were not very old either. 1955 was the date of the oldest. Except for three trains on the London Transport Central Line composed of 1938-built motor coaches and 1920s trailers, the oldest electric multiple-units dated back to 1949. Carriages and wagons had a rather longer lifespan. There were LNER carriages in main-line service and some remained until the 1970s. There were probably some GER wagons. Whilst some lines had modern colour light signalling and automatic train control apparatus, others still had equipment of Great Eastern origin. In fact in some instances the two eras worked together and still do. In 1963 the Great Eastern network was still recognisable.

After 1963, the Beeching Report took effect. 1964 saw a slaughter of branch lines. Other years were a bit less harsh. At the same time BR's 'corporate image' started to emerge. Besides seeing the origins of the current livery, which at present is in the course of being altered. This period also saw a move away from British Railways' rather striking, stylish architecture of the 1950s to the more mundane style of today. The mid-1960s saw the arrival of the Brush Type 4 diesel locomotives. Initiallly these appeared in a rather pleasant two-tone green.

Above:
Massey Bromley's 60 Class E10 0-4-4T locomotives of 1878-1883 were the largest class of that wheel arrangement to be built by GER. On 28 May 1909 No 060 approaches Chantry signalbox with the Fridays only 3.42pm Chelmsford-Braintree. *LCGB*

They are now painted all-over blue, with some sporting silver roofs and red buffer beams. In 1977 two sported Union Jacks down their sides. Some of these locomotives now bear names. October 1984 saw the arrival of the first Class 86 electric locomotives for the Anglian electrification.

What of the future? Electric working of passenger trains to Ipswich using 25kV ac commenced on 13 May 1985. The same day also saw the inauguration of electric trains to North Woolwich using 3rd rail dc. Work is currently being undertaken which will bring electric passenger trains, using 25kV, to Harwich and Southminster in May 1986, and Norwich and Cambridge in May 1987. The autumn of 1988 should see the completion of the 25kV electrification between Stratford and the West Coast main line to enable a certain amount of electric freight working. London Transport has been turned into London Regional Transport. A large part of their Docklands Light Rapid Transit System will be built on or alongside GER lines. The Central Line will in the 1990s be one of the first fully automated railways in Britain. Fenchurch Street and Liverpool Street stations are being rebuilt. What the position on the Great Eastern will be on 31 December 1999 is something that only time can tell.

In the past amongst railway enthusiasts and the travelling public the Great Eastern was not a railway which ranked high in their estimation, nor to some extent does it still today. To take just one example prior to 1943 no one had written a book specifically relating to the GE. In that year the late Mr C. Langley Aldrich produced the first edition of his classic *Locomotives of the Great Eastern Railway*; yet he had to publish it himself. Ironically the result was a sell-out which suggested that there were rather more lovers of

the Great Eastern amongst enthusiasts than had been suspected.

It should not be thought that the Great Eastern got universal criticism in the past — far from it. Before World War 1 the railway received many accolades from writers not only in Great Britain but also abroad. Indeed even today it still receives such accolades; yet equally there were and still are justifiable areas of criticism. Let us now consider everything in more detail.

It must be admitted straight from the start that except for a few years at the beginning of the 1950s when the 'Britannia' 4-6-2s made their appearance and the end of the decade when the English Electric Type 4 diesels first arrived, the Great Eastern lacked glamour. It did not have the showy long distance expresses of the East and West Coast routes to Scotland, nor of the Great Western's West Country route. Equally nor was there the glamour of the 'Dover Mail' or the 'Southern (later Brighton) Belle' over shorter distances. There was not the panache of the Great Central's London expresses, nor the spectacular scenery of the Midland's Scottish express or the London & South Western's Plymouth trains. No — it was an unspectacular line; what the Edwardians called a 55mph sort of line; a line taken by the artist David Weston in his series paintings on the British steam railway to epitomise the Edwardian era. It was an apt choice. The Eastern Counties are a rural area where for many years there was not really any need for any one to travel beyond the next big

13

town. The Great Eastern's crack express away from its continental boat trains was the 'Norfolk Coast Express' which ran only in the summer and that brought the wealthy and the reasonably well off 'foreigners' to the rather posh resorts of the North Norfolk Coast. Since they did not visit the area in winter there was no need for it then. This situation still applies today to some extent. Nor should unspectacular scenery be thought to be a disadvantage. Pleasant scenery often reflects itself on the local inhabitants. Norwich is in my opinion the friendliest city in England.

Another reason for the Great Eastern's lack of glamour was the fact that its two main lines, particularly at their London ends were hardly suited for the speeds obtained by the crack expresses on the Great Western and the East and West Coast main lines. The western main line, particularly south of Cambridge abounds in numerous curves which preclude really fast running such as can be obtained on the rival Great Northern route to Cambridge. The eastern main line besides having severe speed restrictions through Stratford, Chelmsford, Colchester and over the Wensum swing bridge, had the formidable Brentwood and Belstead banks. There was also the problems of the severe weight restrictions imposed by the line's civil engineers. These posed problem for many years to locomotive engineers. Even Sir Nigel Gresley

had to give over the design of the 'B17' 'Sandringham' 4-6-0s to the North British Locomotive Company who were more adept at dealing with such problems. In later years these restrictions were somewhat eased, but only the advent of diesel traction finally saw them vanish.

It should not be thought though these problems coupled with the most restricted loading gauge of any company in the country meant that the Great Eastern's locomotives were underpowered. They were not! Nor when they were given their head were they slow. Cecil J. Allen in his autobiography *Two Million Miles of Train Travel* relates that on his footplate ride on a round top fireboxed 'Claud' (LNER CLass D14) in 1908 hauling the 'Norfolk Coast Express', 70mph was reached twice. He also relates that on another journey he timed a Belpaire fireboxed 'Claud' (LNER Class D15) at 76mph whilst in his *Great Eastern Railway* he gives a record of another 'D15' in 1936 reaching 86mph. Hardly *City of Truro* I agree, but then speed records are isolated exceptions. In the same book Mr Allen also records a rebuilt 'B12' reaching 90mph. The 'B12s' and the 'J15' 0-6-0s were often reckoned to be the Great Eastern's finest engines. The former have been held by some to be the finest express engines to take the metals in this country. Certainly Cecil J. Allen was full of praise for their work on the heavy

'Hook Continental' boat express from Liverpool Street to Parkeston Quay; his description of one journey in 1922 is worth quoting. 'A laggard empty coach train into No 8 platform at Liverpool Street held us up at the start, No 1566 blowing furiously with impatience at the delay. Well, we got away, sighted "distants" at caution at Bridge Box and Romford but got all signals off in time, so storming through the London suburbs to such purpose as to achieve an average of 55mph up the gradual rise to Harold Wood. The 4-6-0 was then attacking Brentwood bank in terrific style when Brentwood Yard Box down distant was seen to be at caution. This time steam had to be shut off and speed dropped by several miles an hour when at last the offending "home" fell to clear.

'Now (Driver "Rocky") Chapman advanced his cut-off to 50 per cent, and with the regulator full open we blasted our way up through Brentwood cutting with a ferocity sufficient to be heard halfway across the county — or so it sounded! Chelmsford in no more than 36½ minutes with such a load was an astonishing time in those days, but now our hard-worked No 1566 could be eased somewhat with the cut-off brought back to 25 per cent and the regulator to the first port only. Eventually we came to a stand at Parkeston Quay in 80¼ minutes from Liverpool Street. . .' Stirling stuff about what was the Great Eastern's hardest job. The 'B12s' greatest merit was their ability to work over lines that other express engines could not, unlike their greatest rivals — the Great Western's 'Saints'. This ability was put to great use in World War 2 when they were used on ambulance trains reaching places previously unvisited by express engines.

The 'J15s' could with very few exceptions go anywhere and do anything. Cecil J. Allen has not recorded any runs behind these extremely useful machines, indeed they were not built for speed. They had started off in 1883 as heavy goods engines and finished in 1962 as light goods engines having at one stage been secondary line

passenger power. Much has been said of them. Even today enginemen remember them with affection. Of course when one thinks about the Great Eastern, one automatically thinks of the 'Jazz' suburban service. When introduced on 12 July 1920 it was described as 'The Last Word in Steam-Operated Suburban Train Services' — the peak of suburban train operation. The aim of the 'Jazz' service very plainly was to increase a suburban service, which in part was charging diabolically low fares, to the maximum extent for the minimum cost. The Great Eastern's suburban lines, particularly those to Enfield and Chingford, were even before 1910 extremely overcrowded and by 1920 shorter working hours had made the rush hours intolerable. Conditions can be best described as equalling the rear carriages of a Central Line tube train following the cancellation of several preceding trains. Those who've experienced this will know what I mean. Chronic overcrowding is the phrase. Understandably some 3rd class passengers got in 2nd class carriages. The railway stationed porters opposite the 1st class to ensure they were not invaded. The only way that the situation could really be improved was by electrification, on which the General Manager Sir Henry Thornton was not prepared to risk shareholders' money, although a suburban electrification scheme was proposed at that time. Thus came about the 'Jazz' service, which by a relatively small number of alterations in the existing equipment in words of Cecil J. Allen increased the down (weekday) service between 5 and 7.30pm by 50 per cent, the down Saturday service, between 12 and 2.30pm by 58 per cent and the up morning service, arriving between 8 and 10am by 75 per cent — an amazing achievement! Although the train service was improved and the quality of the passengers' journey was improved in that they stood more chance of getting a seat, it did not mean that the seats were any more comfortable, not did it mean their journey time was improved — it was only a stop-gap measure and Thornton is reported to have said that electrification would have had to come eventually, which it did.

Much has been said of the Great Eastern's cheap workman's fares which enabled the low-paid to live in the then, more pleasant suburbs rather than in inner London. It must however be remembered that these cheap fares were only available to and from certain stations. For example, whilst they were available to

Above:
The 'S44' class 0-4-4Ts of 1898-1901 were not the most popular of locomotives with firemen as they tended to be rather poor steamers. In GER days they were mainly used on suburban trains. On Sunday 28 November 1909, No 1112 brings the 12.52pm Liverpool Street-Chingford up Bethnal Green bank. *LCGB*

Above right:
Another 'Claud Hamilton', this time No 1881 of 1901 storms up Brentwood bank in the early years of this century on an up express. Both this locomotive and No 1891 seen previously are of the original round-topped firebox variety of 1900. Although an oil burner, this engine has a high sided tender which superseded the round-topped version used on the first batch of 'Clauds' and the 'P43s'. *L&GRP (21320)*

Walthamstow and Enfield they were not available to Chingford and Romford. The Great Eastern had had the cheap fares forced on it by Parliament and whilst it liked to show how well it treated the working man, when it wanted to keep him out of a particular area it made sure that it did. On the Chingford line after Walthamstow, third class fares were abnormally high and second class fares were higher than normal. On the Loughton, Epping and Ongar line workmen's fares were only introduced to Leyton and Leytonstone in 1911 after considerable pressure from the London County Council. The rest of the branch did not have them, and the train services profitted from the GER's policy on fares.

'If' wrote Cecil J. Allen in *The Great Eastern Railway*, 'there was one activity above almost any other on which the Great Eastern Railway was entitled to pride itself, it was the Continental steamer services by way of Harwich'. The railway took great pride in these services. It built the modern port of Harwich for the services and used the connecting trains as its show-pieces. Whilst it could not hope to compete for the lucrative traffic to France and Southern Europe, the Company was able to get a good share of the traffic to Northern and Eastern Europe. It must be said that in many instances the Great Eastern's route was not the quickest, whilst its sea passage was somewhat longer than that of the South Eastern & Chatham and London, Brighton & South Coast railways. Many people liked short

sea journeys and long train journeys, which was something the South Eastern & Chatham, who also competed for Northern Europe made great play of. The Great Eastern however, ran its boats at night enabling people to sleep away the worst part of the journey. The boat trains, if they were for London, had the best carriages and the best engines. The 'Hook Continental' was much more the Pride of the Line than the 'Norfolk Coast Express', as was the Harwich-York train — the 'North Country Continental'. This train provided a very useful cross-country service as well as being reputed to be the first train to

provide meals for third class passengers, allegedly in 1891, although a study of timetables has rather discredited this claim. The real claimant of that honour could well be the London & North Western's 'Scotch Express' (ancestor of the 'Royal Scot').

From a technical viewpoint, the Great Eastern was not particularly brilliant. It is true that it was probably the first railway in the world to make a large scale application of oil fuel, but this was because in the mid-1880s residue from the Company's oil-gas plant at Stratford was fouling the River Lea and the local sanitary authorities did not like it. Necessity being the mother of invention, the Locomotive Superintendent Mr James Holden devised a way of burning the offending residue in locomotive fireboxes. This was all very well, but there was not enough GER-produced oil to supply those engines so equipped and so additional supplies had to be imported. In the 1900s the cost of oil rose and so oil firing was abandoned. It should be pointed out also that only a minority of engines burned oil. Indeed in the great coal strike of the spring of 1912, the Great Eastern's triumph of being the only main line railway to maintain normal services the whole time was due to having brought extra stocks of coal beforehand! Equally it is true that in 1899 the Great Eastern had the distinction of installing Britain's first power signalling at Spital fields goods yard (a McKenzie & Holland & Westinghouse electro-pneumatic

installation); but this was just a one-off job. It has in fact been said that the Great Eastern waited for the patents to run out before installing any new apparatus. Of course it must be pointed out that most of the pre-grouping railways were not particularly technically innovative. Even when they did try something new it was not installed throughout their system. Most of the great technical advances have come since the grouping and nationalisation. In the GER's case practically everything — power signalling, the great hump yards at March, electrification. But the Great Eastern had a case — lack of money. The Great Eastern was a practical line, it did not promise or attempt what it could not achieve. It was the first railway to use an illuminated white fish-tail against a distance signal at night to assist enginemen. It was also the first railway to fit its express engines with steam heating hoses at the front end. Very useful on a cold winter's day if an engine already turned brought the empty carriages for a train into a terminus; small things but of practical use. There was one area where the Great Eastern was held to be above all — the treatment of its staff. Certainly for its day the Great Eastern was a good employer. Staff were treated better than on other lines. Of course, the unions were not recognised, but then the Chairman, Lord Claud Hamilton, regarded them as an interference between employer and staff. Certainly there existed a very cordial relationship and co-operation between company and staff.

The GER was the first railway to introduce a pension scheme for employees, it also gave part-paid holidays and generally wages were higher than elsewhere. There was of course another side to the coin and there were those who regarded the railway as a bad employer. Certainly hours were long and conditions could be bad. Signalboxes could be very draughty places, a 'J15' might not seem such a wonderful engine when working tender-first across the Fens on a cold bleak January night, and the working conditions in some locomotive sheds were unspeakable!

The Great Eastern's attitude to passenger comfort was rather interesting. Railways always tended to treat main-line passengers better than their suburban counterpart, but in the GER's case this difference was rather extreme. Obviously first class passengers had the best accommodation, even on suburban trains they had a carpet on the floor. Second class accommodation in the twentieth century was only on suburban and boat trains. However the difference between a main-line third and a suburban third was enormous. The former was more luxurious than today's firsts on the Venice-Simplon Orient Express while the latter were very hygienic. No cushions just bare boards. The GER's main-line third fares were not exorbitant.

What effect did the GER have on East Anglia? Quite a lot. Certainly it was responsible for both the development of the east coast holiday resorts of Great Yarmouth, Lowestoft, Cromer, Felixstowe, Hunstanton, Walton-on-the-Naze and Clacton, but not Southend. It was also in part responsible for the development of the eastern commuter belt, in consequence destroying a lot of good countryside. During the great agricultural depression it also tried ways of persuading farmers to develop new crops. In fact during World War 1 it ran a farm. Finally it started the first motor-bus services in East Anglia.

What effect did the Railway have on literature? Not much, but then railways aren't suppose to influence writers. Nevertheless the Great Eastern may probably keep alive the name of Richard Austin Freeman and his detective Dr John Evelyn Thorndyke (the ace of scientific detectives) through the Case of Oscar Brodski. A story involving the murder of a man and the subsequent placing of his body on the line to make it appear as if he had been killed by a train.

The setting is believed to be Manningtree. The story is occasionally reprinted.

It is also of note that the Great Eastern Railway was possibly the only English railway to influence the decision of no less a person than the Pope! During late 1916 and early 1917 when consideration was being given to establishing a Roman Catholic Diocese for Essex it was proposed that the Cathedral should be in Chelmsford however the Bishop elect Monseigneur Bernard Ward being a railway enthusiast wanted it at Ilford; Stratford being out doubtless as being too close to Westminster. Rome said Chelmsford. Ward felt Ilford was the right place as it had main line, suburban, Southend and Chigwell Loop trains. Chelmsford only had a mine line service. Eventually a compromise of Brentwood was reached — this being because here you had only Chigwell Loop trains missing. The new bishop was not adverse to arriving at a Parish on the footplate. Over the years Great Eastern enthusiasts have bcome bolder than in earlier days. Certainly the infant British Railways gave the GER a boost by using it to show off the new 'Britannia' 4-6-2s and later as the first line to be rid of steam. As years passed, so interest in the Company grew and in 1973 the Great Eastern Railway Society was formed in Chelmsford to promote a widespread awareness of the railway both through modelling and practical research. The Society's headquarters are at the North Woolwich Station Museum. Each March the Society has its Annual General Meeting at Stratford whilst each October there is a half-yearly meeting held at a venue somewhere on the system. The Society has been responsible for two major exhibitions and one book. It produces a quarterly magazine — *Great Eastern Journal*, whilst there are also information sheets produced on various subjects of interest such as timetables, locomotives and the minutes of the Company's various committees.

In writing this book I would like to thank Messrs John Plume, Bernard Walsh and Nigel Bowdidge for their comments and suggestions; my mother Mrs Margaret Phillips for her patience; also Graham Stacey, custodian of the LCGB Ken Nunn Collection for allowing me special access to the collection. The staff of the publishers for their help.

Charles Phillips

Tye Green, Stock
Essex
15 July 1985

18

Below:
In the author's opinion this is perhaps the most attractive photograph taken on the GER by the brothers Ken and Christopher Nunn. It shows a Belpaire firebox-fitted 'Claud Hamilton' No 1841 passing Ingatestone station on the 7.03am Clacton-Liverpool Street on 7 May 1910. This view was taken from the signalbox and presents a good picture of a rather pleasant station during the Edwardian era.
LCGB

Below centre:
A nice picture of a Great Eastern coal train hauled by one of the 'F48' class 0-6-0s, No 1180 near Thoby in October 1910. The 'F48s' were the goods equivalent of the round-topped firebox 'Clauds'. The train is the 2.35pm March-Wickford. *LCGB*

Bottom:
At Ingrebourne signalbox in June 1915, 'G58' No 1224 passes with the Peterborough-Aldersbrook (Ilford) coal train via Ipswich. The 'G58s' were the Belpaire firebox version of the 'F48' class. *LCGB*

19

Left:
The 'Y14' was undoubtedly the Great Eastern's most useful class. These photographs illustrate some of the varied duties which they performed. In this view a dual air- and vacuum-braked member of the class, No 557, heads an excursion train formed of Great Northern carriages from St Albans-Southend through Brentwood station in July 1909. *LCGB*

Below left:
The Great Eastern used to paint its carriages at Felixstowe, which necessitated the running of special trains from Stratford works. 'Y14' No 555 is seen on such a duty passing Ingrebourne signalbox. *LCGB*

Bottom left:
In May 1908, 'Y14' No 537 is seen near Brentwood with the 5.50pm Colchester-Tufnel Park cattle train. *LCGB*

Below:
An interesting photograph showing what the GER provided its enginemen with for protection when running tender-first. 'Y14' No 865 with the 4.30am Goodmayes-Chelmsford goods leaving Brentwood on 22 March 1911. *LCGB*

Bottom:
Finally, what is believed to be the only existing photograph of a 'Y14' in Railway Operating Division service in France during World War 1; No 534 (GER and ROD number) at Mondicourt South box on a ration van train on 9 October 1918. *LCGB*

Above:
The 'N31' was a variant of the 'Y14', but they were not very successful for a number of reasons, mainly due to the setting of the steam chests and valves. All disappeared by the end of 1925, unlike the 'Y14s', which lasted until 1962. Sometime before World War 1, No 948 is seen passing Stratford on an up goods. *LCGB*

Below:
What the Great Eastern called the 'M15' class 2-4-2T and the London & North Eastern Railway called the 'F4' and 'F5' classes was of almost equal value to the company as the 'Y14'. No 235 is seen leaving Thorpe-le-Soken with a local train for Clacton circa 1910. *Real Photographs Co (T7998)*

Top right:
Although the Great Eastern did not use tank locomotives in quite the same way that the London, Brighton & South Coast did, they were in some instances used for quite lengthy journeys. On

4 August 1909, No 235 is seen passing Warren Hill platform Newmarket with the 2.30pm Haughley-Cambridge, a run of 40 miles. Warren Hill is of interest as it was used only for the Newmarket Races. *LCGB*

Centre right:
To many people, however, the 'M15s' were always suburban engines and will be remembered as such. Towards the end of the Great Eastern's existence, No 679 is seen at Gidea Park with a local train composed of the latest suburban bogie stock. *L&GRP (16325)*

Bottom right:
The side window cab version of the 'M15' was the 'G69' (later LNER Class F6) and in their early days they were very definitely suburban locomotives. In 1921 No 68 arrives at Gidea Park with a local train for Liverpool Street. This is composed of bogie carriages constructed using the bodies of four-wheelers on new underframes. *L&GRP (16350)*

Top:
The 'C32' was a tank engine version of the 'T26' 2-4-0 and before World War 1 the class was kept to outer suburban duties such as London-Chelmsford, upon which duty No 1060 is seen leaving Brentwood in May 1908. *LCGB*

Above:
The Great Eastern for some reason did not take up the railmotor like other companies and instead in 1909 produced a light branch 2-4-2T, the 'Y65'. Amongst other lines which they at one time worked was the Witham-Braintree branch which on Fridays in 1910 had a through working to Chelmsford, where No 1304 is seen waiting to leave with the return working to Braintree. *LCGB*

Top:
I include this photograph, on the Churchbury Loop taken in March 1915, to show what the front of a GER auto train driving trailer looked like. The first Great Eastern service to be operated by auto trains was the Mildenhall branch in 1913. *LCGB*

Above:
The 'Norfolk Coast Express' was the Great Eastern's ace. In July 1909 the train is seen leaving Liverpool Street for Cromer behind round-top firebox 'Claud Hamilton' No 1870. *LCGB*

Top:
The Great Eastern did not possess all that many water troughs. The best-known were near Ipswich, where Belpaire firebox-fitted 'Claud' No 1823 is seen taking water on the 1.00pm Cromer-Liverpol Street in September 1910. *LCGB*

Above:
In the same month, the same train is seen headed by 'Claud' No 1816 crossing Trowse swing bridge. *LCGB*

Top right:
The exchanging of mails whilst moving is not something that is normally associated with the Great Eastern. Furthermore it is not an operation which was easily photographed as it usually took place after dark. However, on 10 June 1908 near Brentwood, the 3.30pm Ipswich-Liverpool Street is seen doing so, hauled by 'Claud' No 1855. *LCGB*

Above right:
'Clauds' were nothing if not adaptable. On 30 October 1912 a dual brake fitted locomotive, No 1892, is seen near Northumberland Park with a Whitemoor-Spitalfields fitted goods. *LCGB*

Right:
The 'T19s' were built between 1886 and 1897, but by 1902, had been superseded on regular main line duties by the 'Clauds'. In 1902-04 some of them were rebuilt with a large Belpaire boiler, side window cab and a brass-capped chimney. These locomotives were rather front heavy in appearance and were nicknamed 'Humpty Dumpties'. No 1034 is seen passing Harold Wood on a Liverpool Street-Norwich train in 1908. *LCGB*

Below:

In 1905-08 a total of 60 unrebuilt 'T19s' were rebuilt into a 4-4-0 version of the 'Humpty Dumpties'. The first converted (No 1035) ran for several years in a grey livery so that the whole of the 4-4-0 rebuild class became known as 'Dolly Greys'. No 719 is seen passing Bethnal Green with the 11.05am Liverpool Street-Hunstanton on 12 August 1909. *LCGB*

Bottom:

Seen near Lakenham in 1923 is 'T26' No 492 on a passenger train. The number on the tender was part of the train control system adopted from the Midland Railway. The 'T26' was a mixed traffic version of the 'T19'. *L&GRP (20157)*

Right:

The Great Eastern's breakdown train passing through Brentwood en route from Stratford to Walton with what appears to be part of a turntable, behind 'T26' class No 1252 in April 1911. *LCGB*

Below right:

In the early days of World War 1 during 1914, 'T26' No 1253 passes Thoby box with a Colchester (St Botolphs)-Plymouth troop train carrying cavalry and their mounts. *LCGB*

Bottom right:

Later to become LNER Class Y5, diminutive 0-4-0ST No 209, the first member of GER '209' class is seen here during Great Eastern days. This locomotive was a Neilson product of 1874. *Real Photographs Co (C4072)*

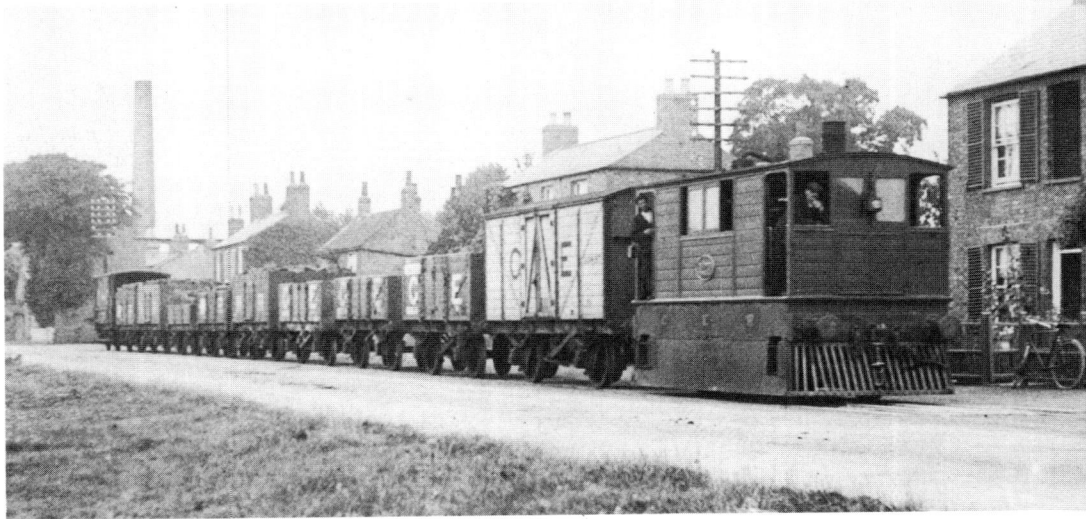

Top left:
The Kelvedon, Tiptree & Tollesbury Light Railway, although only a branch of the Great Eastern, managed to achieve a notoriety equal to Colonel Stephens' legendary light railways. At a level crossing near Kelvedon on Thursday 31 March 'R24' class 0-6-0T No 391 waits with the 12.30pm Kelvedon-Tollesbury whilst the guard closes the crossing gates. The crossing was a headache to motorists in later years as it was on the main London-Colchester road. The locomotive has the front section of the coupling rods removed because of the sharp curves on the line, and is therefore technically a 2-4-0T. *LCGB*

Above left:
The Great Eastern built two types of tram engine. The 'G15' (LNER Class Y6) which was 0-4-0T design, and the 'C53' (LNER Class J70) which was a 0-6-0T. This photograph shows an 0-4-0T tram No 127 on the famed Wisbech & Upwell Tramway with a goods train in Elm Road, Wisbech, on 27 July 1912. *LCGB*

Bottom left:
Although tram engines were mainly used on the Wisbech & Upwell Tramway, they also performed shunting duties on the GER's numerous quays.

With the exception of a couple of locomotives on the Great Northern, the Great Eastern was the only company to operate tram engines. Seen shunting on Ipswich quay on 30 April 1910 is 'C53' class No 130, built new in that year. *LCGB*

Top:
Away from the Great Western Railway, it can be argued that the Great Eastern's 'S69' class 4-6-0s (better known to many as LNER Class B12) were the most successful of all the English pre-grouping 4-6-0 designs. They were essentially 4-4-0s with an extra coupled axle and as such they were Fred V. Russell's masterpiece. Although main-line locomotives, from their earliest days they also worked on the Southend line, as this view of No 1504 at Brentwood on its maiden day in traffic in May 1912 shows. *LCGB*

Above:
The 10 'E72' class 0-6-0 locomotives appeared in 1912. In April 1914 No 1241 passes Thoby box with a Peterborough-Aldersbrook coal train. This train is following the honoured GER route from Peterborough to London, a route used by the only through passenger trains between Liverpool Street and Peterborough, ie via Ely, Bury St Edmunds, Ipswich, Chelmsford and Brentwood. *LCGB*

Above:
The 'L77' 0-6-2Ts were the Great Eastern's most powerful suburban locomotives except for the unique 'Decapod'. The first two came out in 1915, followed by a further 10 in 1921. At the time of the Grouping another 10 were under construction. No 1006 brings a Chelmsford-Liverpol Street train into Gidea Park in 1922. *L&GRP (16358)*

Below:
Much has been made of the Great Eastern's connections with the Northern Lines. Here for a change is a GER train on the South Eastern & Chatham Railway. The date is 7 May 1910, the place is Hither Green exchange sidings, and 'S44' No 1115 is just arriving with a freight train from Spitfields via the East London Railway. *LCGB*

Top right:
Obviously the Great Eastern and the South Eastern & Chatham had a very good relationship as nothing less than one of the latter's famous 'D' class 4-4-0 locomotives, No 740, is seen at Liverpool Street in 1912 with a royal train from Dover to Wolferton. *LCGB*

Centre right:
The great bulk of Holden's remarkable 'Decapod' is apparent in this side view of the unique locomotive when new at Stratford works. *LPC*

Bottom right:
Even when 'rebuilt' into 0-8-0 tender locomotive, the former 'Decapod' was a massive looking engine. It is seen here in 1913. *LCGB*

Top:
**One of the three 'D' crane tanks seen on the
turntable at Stratford works circa 1909.** *LCGB*

Above:
**A fine view of GER Holden 'G58' class 0-6-0
No 1213 of 1905 in austerity grey livery. This design
became LNER Class J17, the final example being
withdrawn by British Railways in 1962.** *LPC (0788)*

Top right:
**The last GER design was the 'H88' class 'Super
Clauds'; all of the new locomotives appearing in
1923 after the grouping. On 5 July 1924 No 1787E
(the letter E representing Great Eastern section) in
LNER livery waits to leave Liverpool Street for
Southend. Under the LNER these locomotives
became Class D16.** *LCGB*

Above right:
**A period-piece view of Class D15 'Claud Hamilton'
No 8883 and Class F3 (GER 'C32' class) 2-4-2T
No 8088 at Cromer shed.** *LPC (10864)*

Bottom right:
**The London & North Eastern allocated 20 of
Gresley's 'K2' class 2-6-0 locomotives to the GE
section in the early days of the Grouping. Some at
least, turned up in full Great Northern livery. In the
late 1930s an unidentified member of the class is
seen running light at Colchester.** *Lens of Sutton*

34

Below:
To help with moving coal traffic from the north, a number of ex-Great Central '04' class 2-8-0s were sent to the GE section. No 6204 was caught on an up goods near Great Chesterford in 1935.
Real Photographs Co (23768)

Bottom:
During the widening of Brentwood station from two to four tracks, Class B17 No 2822 *Alnwick Castle* gingerly makes its way past with the 'Flushing Continental'. This train has in its formation three Pullman cars. *Real Photographs Co*

Top right:
Approaching Harold Wood, another 'B17' 4-6-0, No 2831 *Serlby Hall* is seen on a down express after widening to four tracks has been completed.
Real Photographs Co (T5526)

Centre right:
One of the two streamlined 'B17s', No 2859 *East Anglian* near Chadwell Heath on the up 'East Anglian' in 1939. *Real Photographs Co (23872)*

Bottom right:
With 289 members, the humble Class J39 0-6-0 was Sir Nigel Gresley's most numerous class and on the GE section undertook most duties. In 1939 No 1984 is seen at the head of a down goods near Chadwell Heath. *Real Photographs Co (23891)*

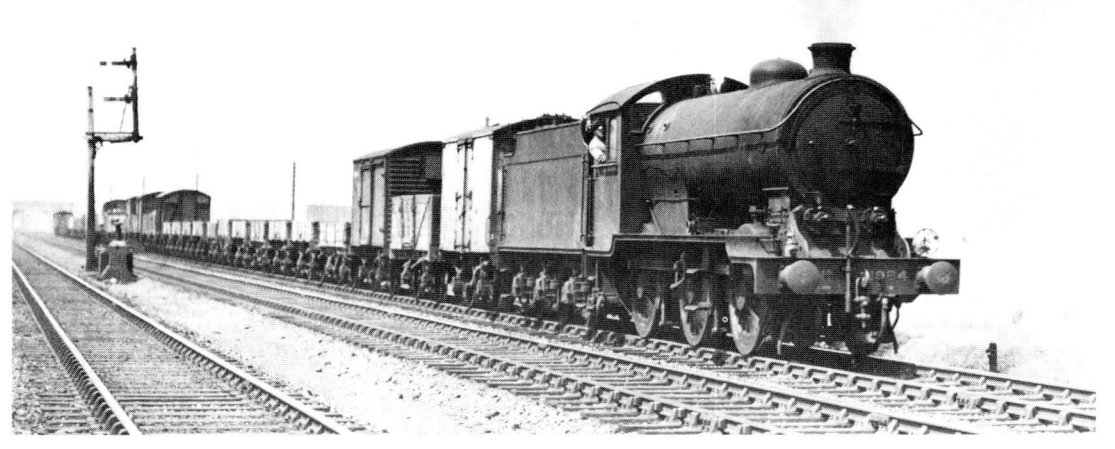

Top left:
The main passenger work for 'J39s' was on the Southend line. With a formation of ex-GER suburban bogie stock, No 2729 leaves Brentwood for Southend during the widening of the station.
Real Photographs Co (T6310)

Centre left:
In 1945, just after the end of the war in Europe, No 299 is seen near Trumpington with a Cambridge-Liverpool Street train. *Real Photographs Co (23894)*

Bottom left:
To the Great Eastern section fell the honour of owning what were probably Britain's last steam tram engines. Two locomotives of the Class Y10 were built by Sentinel in 1930 for the Wisbech & Upwell Tramway, but they were not altogether

successful and soon gravitated to the Great Yarmouth quay lines where No 8404 is seen in 1939 complete with a crew of four. *Lens of Sutton*

Top:
'Y4' class 0-4-0T No 7210 seen at work in LNER days. This class originated as class 'B74' on the GER, being a design by Hill introduced in 1913, the final example disappearing in 1963.
Real Photographs Co

Above:
Ex-Great Central Class D9 4-4-0 No 6028 pilots Class D15 No 8896 on a local train of former GER stock at King's Lynn in June 1938. The 'D9s' undertook a number of duties on the GE section in the 1930s, including the Peterborough mails.
R. F. Roberts

'C14' class 4-4-2T No 6128, one of five members of this former Great Central Railway class allocated to the GE section, is seen near Ipswich in 1938 on a semi-fast working. *Photomatic*

Between 1931 and 1937 nine ex-North Eastern Class J21 0-6-0s worked on the Great Eastern lines. Essentially a NER version of the 'J15' (they were both designed by T. W. Worsdell), they did not find favour with the GER men. In June 1936 No 300 was recorded at Dereham. *H. C. Casserley*

Besides reclassifying the 'S69' 4-6-0s as 'B12', the LNER decided that it wanted to 'improve' them. One modification tried was fitting them with ACFI water feed heating apparatus as seen on No 8527 on an up Cambridge train near Trumpington in 1934.

The men promptly christened these locomotives 'Hikers'. The Great North of Scotland lines got some 'B12s' and gave them the same name because it was a long hike from the tender to the firebox. *Real Photographs Co (23714)*

The next alteration was rebuilding with larger round-top firebox boilers as seen in this photograph of No 8585 on an up Norwich restaurant car train near Chadwell Heath in 1938. *Real Photographs Co (23717)*

The same treatment was also applied to the 'Claud Hamiltons' as this shot of No 8849 on a down Walton special near Chadwell Heath shows. The LNER classified these locomotives 'D16/3'. *Real Photographs Co (23739)*

Below:
An official LNER photograph of the lengthened Primrose Street bridge outside Liverpool Street station in February 1939, with the front end of a 'B12' visible on the approach road to the fully decked turntable. *British Railways*

Bottom:
Belpaire firebox 'Claud', Class D15 No 8842 on an up express on Brentwood bank on 15 July 1939.

Below:
At Wells-on-Sea on 29 June 1939, Class D13 (formerly 'T19') 4-4-0 No 8030 heads a local service. *H. C. Casserley*

Bottom:
'B12' No 8535 prior to being rebuilt is seen on an express in 1929. *Real Photographs Co (23715)*

Below:
At Wells-on-Sea on 29 June 1939, Class D13 (formerly 'T19') 4-4-0 No 8030 heads a local service. *H. C. Casserley*

Bottom:
'B12' No 8535 prior to being rebuilt is seen on an express in 1929. *Real Photographs Co (23715)*

Above:
The LNER reclassified the 'Y14s' as Class J15. In 1937 No 7538 leaves Ipswich on an up engineer's train. *Photomatic*

Below:
Throughout the 'Big Four' period the 'J15s' remained in Great Eastern territory. Sometime during the 1930s, No 7645 is seen on an excursion train of six-wheelers. *Real Photographs Co (R7157)*

Above:
The LNER reclassified the 'T26' 2-4-0s as Class E4 and at the end of the company's existence, 18 were still in service. In March 1948 No 2790 starts away from Cambridge. *LCGB*

Below:
A Class J17 (former GER 'F48') 0-6-0 No 8221 on a coal train composed in the main of private owner wagons, near Colchester.
Real Photographs Co (T5923)

Below:

The 'J20s' were the Great Eastern's largest 0-6-0s. They were also until 1942 the most powerful locomotives of that wheel arangement in the country. They were mostly used on coal trains between Yorkshire and London, and continued in this role until the 1950s despite the arrival of larger locomotives. In 1935 No 8285 is seen near Great Chesterford with an up coal train.
Real Photographs Co (23757)

Bottom:

Throughout the period 1923-48, the Great Eastern's 2-4-2Ts played a major role in the system's suburban traffic. On 3 April 1937, 'F6' No 7010 arrives at Grange Hill on the Fairlop loop with a train for Fenchurch Street.   *H. C. Casserley*

Top:
In 1930 another member of the class, No 7067, arrives at Hertford East with a train comprising four GER bogie suburban carriages and a main line gas-lit Clerestory as first vehicle. *L&GRP*

Above:
At Ongar in 1938, 'F5' No 7144 prepares to leave for Liverpool Street with a three carriage train. At Epping more carriages will be added to the train. Another 'F5', No 7147, waits on the shed road.
H. C. Casserley

Below:

In addition to suburban work, 2-4-2Ts also operated the passenger services on branch and cross-country lines. At the beautiful Maldon East station in April 1949, 'F5' No 7189 (under the 1946 renumbering scheme, formerly 7142) waits with a Witham train of three ex-GER coaches. The station still exists but the branch line is no more. *Real Photographs Co*

Below:

In addition to suburban work, 2-4-2Ts also operated the passenger services on branch and cross-country lines. At the beautiful Maldon East station in April 1949, 'F5' No 7189 (under the 1946 renumbering scheme, formerly 7142) waits with a Witham train of three ex-GER coaches. The station still exists but the branch line is no more. *Real Photographs Co*

Bottom:

In the late 1930s, 'F3' class 2-4-2T No 8080 leaves Beccles bunker-first with the Lowestoft portion of the combined Yarmouth and Lowestoft train. *Real Photographs Co*

Below:
The classic shot of the Kelvedon, Tiptree & Tollesbury Light Railway in its later years. On 26 June 1948, 'J69' class 0-6-0T No 8636 (post-1946 number, formerly 7090) waits at Tollesbury with its train for Kelvedon. *H. C. Casserley*

Bottom:
The 'N7' was the only GER design that the LNER built in any large numbers, although at no time did it ever completely dominate the Great Eastern suburban services. In 1938 No 833 is seen near Chadwell Heath on a down Shenfield train consisting of two-sets of 'quint-arts'.
Real Photographs Co (23725)

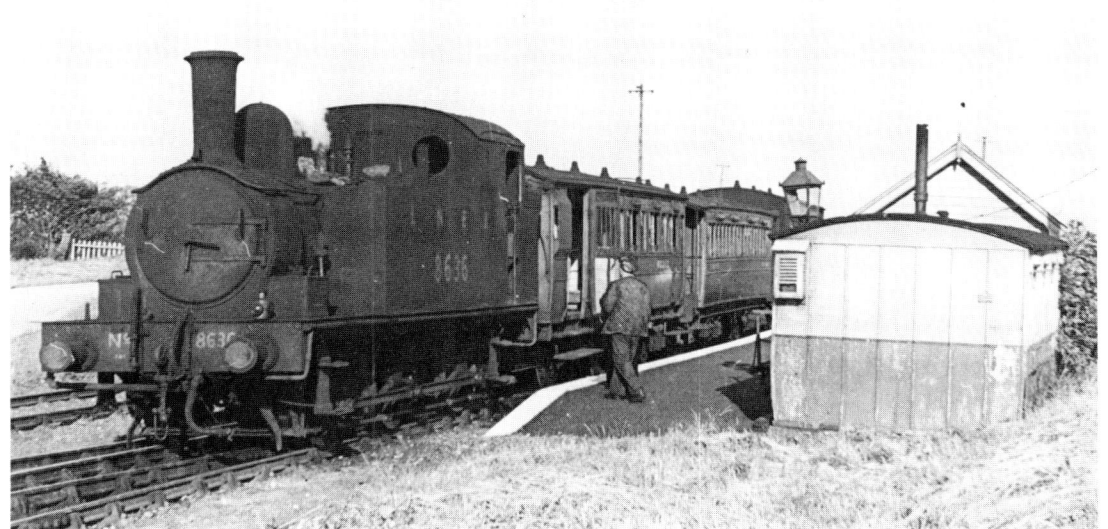

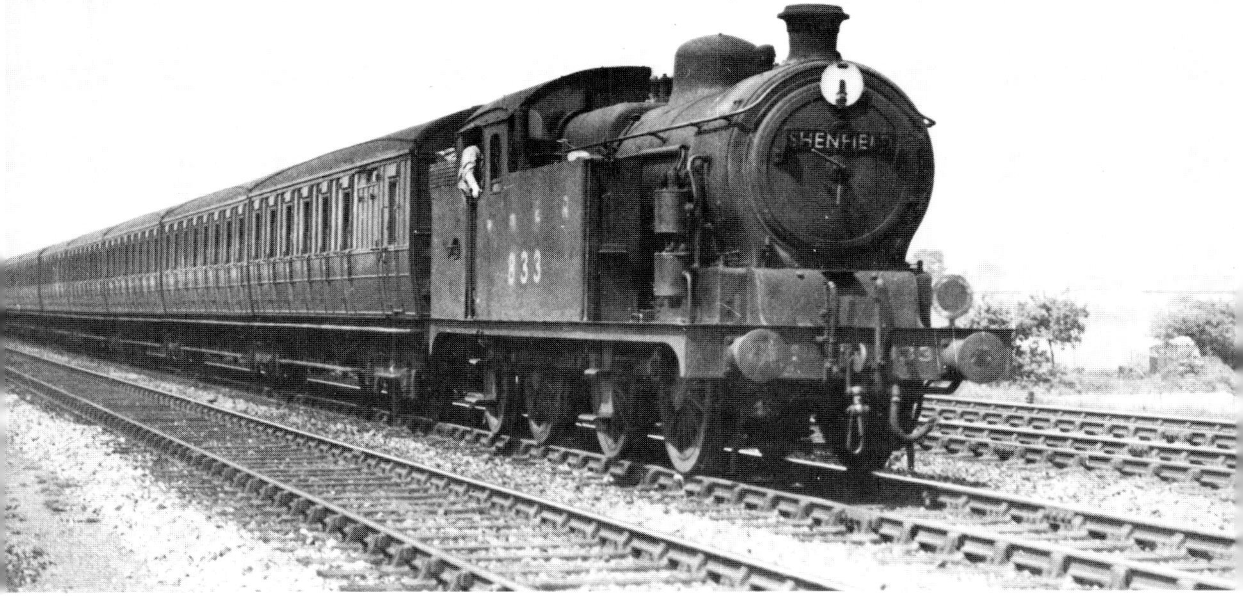

Left:
The 0-6-0T tram locomotives became LNER Class J70. No 7139 has had its side plates removed, but not its cowcatchers and is shunting in Ipswich docks. *Photomatic*

Below left:
The 'V1' and 'V3' class 2-6-2Ts came to the GE section in 1939 and worked on such routes as London to Southend, Clacton and Cambridge, also Norwich to Cromer and Sheringham. In 1948 they were tried out on the Manningtree-Harwich branch. On 2 October of that year No 7680 (post-1946 number) heads a Harwich-Manningtree train on Manningtree south curve. *G. R. Mortimer*

Below right:
The 'V4' class was Sir Nigel Gresley's last design and came out in 1941 shortly before his death. Essentially designed for peacetime conditions they appeared during World War 2, and conseqently their impact was not what it might have been. After a short period on the GE section they were moved to Scotland. No 3401 *Bantam Cock* is seen with a down Cambridge express near Trumpington in 1941. *Real Photographs Co (23842)*

Bottom right:
Although one member of the class reached the Great Eastern lines before World War 2, the ex-GNR 'C12' class 4-4-2T's arrival really belong to those dark days. No 4509 is seen on the Saffron Walden branch near Audley End in 1941. These locomotives ran this branch from that year until 1951.
Real Photographs Co (23627)

Below:
Taken somewhere on the GE section in 1943 or 1944; this photograph shows No 1703 of March shed, one of the many US Army Transportation Corps 'S160' class 2-8-0s which ran in this country for a short time during those difficult days. In the background is No 2364 of Stratford. *Lens of Sutton*

Bottom:
The 'O6' class was better known to LMS men as the Stanier '8F'. The LNER's machines were built by the Southern Railway and remained with the LNER until 1947 when they were loaned to the LMSR. In their short time on the LNER (1944-47) they were renumbered. No 3547 carrying 3147 on the smokebox door was photographed at Stratford in 1947. *Photomatic*

Right:
The War Department 2-8-0s first appeared on loan on the GE section in 1943. After the war, the LNER purchased 200 and classified them 'O7'. Some of these locomotives were intended to replace the 'O6s' loaned to the LMSR. In August 1947, No 3035 (LNER number) of March depot hauls an up freight through Ipswich. *G. R. Mortimer*

Below right:
Edward Thompson's 'B1' class 4-6-0s first reached the GE section in 1943. In July 1947 No 1149 heads the up 'Hook Continental' near Wrabness. *C. B. Herbert*

Below:
The first 'L1' class 2-6-4T came out in 1945, but then no more were built until 1948. At Shenfield in June 1948 the wires are up for the coming electrification as No 67710 on an up Southend train passes No 67703. *H. C. Casserley*

Bottom:
The Great Eastern line's first electric trains were operated by London Transport as part of the Central Line. This photograph taken at Snaresbrooke some time from 1948 onwards shows a train of pre-1935 or standard tube stock on a Woodford working. *IA Library*

Top:
As the Central Line was extended eastward, so the steam service became restricted on the electrified section to goods and a few early-morning trains for staff and on Sundays only for the public. In August 1949 only the Loughton-Ongar section still had regular steam services when 'F5' No 67211 was photographed near Theydon Bois on a train for **Epping.** *Photomatic*

Above:
Although the Central Line was mainly operated by standard tube stock, the six cars of flat-fronted 1935 experimental stock were also used. It was intended that they should be used on the Ongar section but this was not electrified until 1957. In the meantime they undertook other duties for LT including from 1952-54 operating a Loughton-Epping shuttle to supplement the main through service. During this time the photograph was taken at Epping. 'F5' No 67207 is seen on the Epping-Ongar shuttle.
Lens of Sutton

Above:
'A5' class 4-6-2T No 69835, a LNER built locomotive to a former Great Central design, heads the 8.44am Liverpool Street-Southend passing Ilford flyover on Saturday 21 April 1951. *R. E. Vincent*

Below:
The first electric trains began running from Liverpool Street to Shenfield in September 1949. In the following month, unit No 36 leads a nine car train out of Gidea Park towards Liverpool Street. *LCGB*

Top right:
Bo-Bo electric locomotive No 26510 was built in 1914 for the North Eastern Railway's Newport-Shildon mineral line electrification. After this line reverted to steam in 1935, this locomotive and the others in its class were stored. In 1941 the engine was rebuilt as a banker on the Wath incline as part of the Manchester-Sheffield electrification scheme. It never got there and instead ended up as Ilford depot shunter. In November 1950 it took part in some trials of electric stock on the GE section. This view shows it heading a nine-car multiple unit train near Chadwell Heath. *LCGB*

Centre right:
Besides seeing the inauguration of the Shenfield electrification, 1949 also witnessed the first use of a 4-6-2 locomotive on the Great Eastern main lines out of Liverpool Street when former Southern Railway 'Battle of Britain' No 34059 *Sir Archibald Sinclair* ran trials during the spring. The locomotive is seen leaving Norwich (Thorpe) on the 'Norfolkman'. *LCGB*

Below right:
The 'Britannia' class 4-6-2s first made their appearance in the spring of 1951. On 6 June of that year, No 70006 *Robert Burns* enters Liverpool Street with the up 'East Anglian'. Next to the locomotive is a dynamometer car. *LCGB*

Top:
One of the useful former War Department 'Austerity' 2-8-0 locomotives, No 90085 makes good progress with an up coal train near Mountnessing in September 1951.
Real Photos (23366)

Above:
Five members of the LMSR Ivatt Class 2 light 2-6-0 were allocated by British Railways to the GE section. On 20 April 1960, No 46467 brings the Mildenhall branch goods into Barnwall Junction station. In July 1962 five members of the British Railways version of this class were allocated to Stratford. *G. D. King*

Top:
The arrival of electric trains meant that a number of suburban tank locomotives were displaced to the country districts. On 12 September 1951, 'F6' No 67224 leaves Reepham.
E. Tuddenham M&GN Circle

Above:
At Aldeburgh during the time of the famous festival, 'F6' No 67239 waits to depart. *L&GRP (25861)*

Left:
Class N7 No 69707 heads the 3.15pm Class C Sunday milk train from North Elham to Ilford near the start of its journey. *E. Tuddenham M&GN Circle*

Below left:
In the spring of 1951, Class D16 No 62581 is seen near Reepham on the 2.33pm Wroxham-Dereham. This was one of the many former express locomotives relegated to the country by the arrival of the 'B1s' and the 'Britannias'.
E. Tuddenham M&GN Circle

Bottom left:
In November 1953 another 'D16', No 62567 leaves Cambridge with a Newmarket service.
Real Photos (K2063)

Below:
By 1955 the main duties for 'B12s' out of Liverpool Street were the Southend trains, although this service was shared with 'B1s', 'B17s', the occasional 'L1' and virtually everything else at times. No 61557 arrives at Wickford is February of that year with a train for Southend.
Real Photos (K2458)

Bottom:
The 'B12s' also worked through London-Southminster trains. On 19 March 1955, No 61546 has been turned out prior to taking a through train to Liverpool Street. *H. C. Casserley*

Above:

Like the Southend services, the Clacton trains also saw a variety of motive power. In 1950, 'B1' No 61109 leaves Clacton for Liverpool Street. *Real Photos (T5440)*

Below:

Pride of the Great Eastern section steam fleet were the 'Britannia' Pacifics. No 70035 *Rudyard Kipling* is seen on an up Cambridge line express near Broxbourne in July 1955. *Real Photos (23347)*

Above right:

In 1958 Class B17 No 61663 *Everton*, one of the batch named after football clubs, waits to leave Walton for Thorpe. *Hugh Davies*

Centre right:

The Felixstowe branch was slightly special and was the only line away from the London suburban services to receive 'L1s'. In 1956, No 67702 arrives at Felixstowe Town with a train from Ipswich, whilst No 67705 on the right awaits its next duty. *H. C. Casserley*

Below right:

At various times from the late 1920s onwards, members of Class N2 found their way on to the GE lines, although they were more at home on their native Great Northern; at the same time 'N7s' had reached some of that section's sheds. In 1955, No 69561 waits at Harwich town with a Manningtree train. *Photomatic*

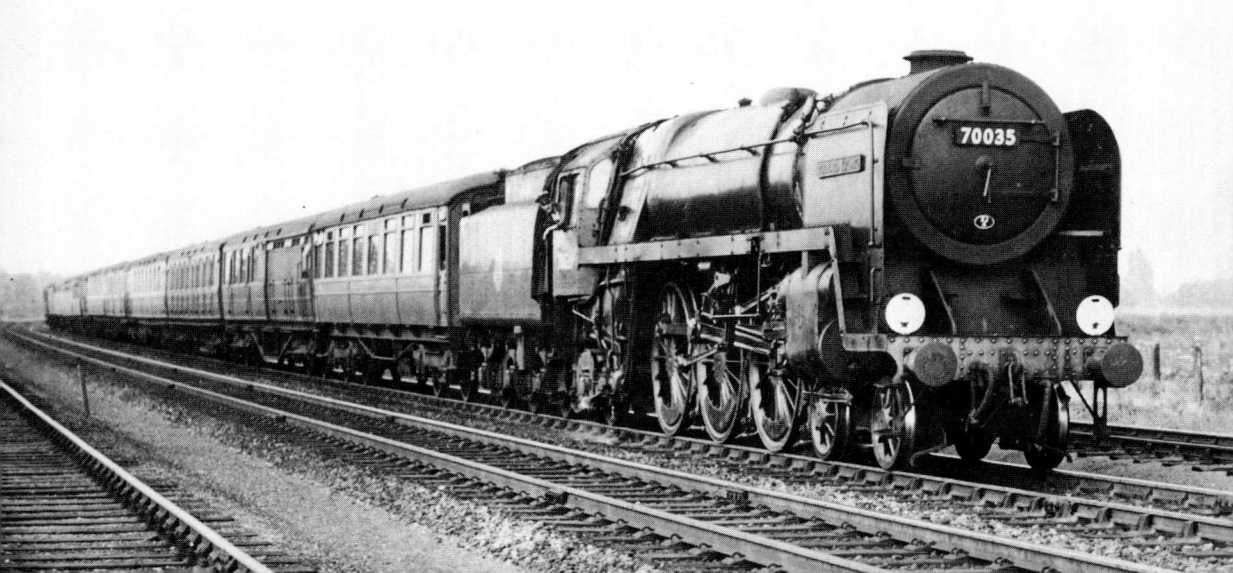

Top left:
Class J17 No 65580 at Audley End with a down goods in September 1959. This train is typical of the mixed goods which had for so long been a part of the railway scene, but which would be extinct within a decade. *Real Photos (23353)*

Above left:
'E4' No 62796 is turned at Mildenhall on 22 September 1956. At this time Mildenhall was a town of contrasts. At the American air base were the latest jet fighters, yet at the railway station the train was something out of Edwardian England. One wonders what the railway enthusiasts among the airmen thought. *H. C. Casserley*

Left:
Another 'E4' at Mildenhall, this time No 62781. This locomotive had a side-windowed cab fitted when it and five other members of the class were tried on the Darlington-Penrith line in the 1930s. The photograph was taken in April 1949. *Real Photos*

Top:
Class J15 No 65391 heads a Bury St Edmunds-Long Melford train at Welnetham on 23 March 1954. The locomotive has a side-windowed cab which was fitted by the LNER for working the Colne Valley & Halstead Railway in Essex. *D. Thompson*

Above:
'J15' No 65455 arrives at Bartlow in August 1957 on a Stour Valley line train. The signalman waits to hand over the tablet for the next section, whilst the fireman has just thrown the tablet for the previous section on to the catcher. A scene epitomising the English country railway in the 1950s. *Hugh Davies*

Above:
The up platform at Elsenham station with the stock of the 2.28pm train to Thaxted standing in the branch platform on 29 August 1952. *R. E. Vincent*

Below:
The Thaxted branch had the distinction of being the last railway opened by the Great Eastern when it was completed in 1913. In June 1951, Class J69 No 68530 starts away from Thaxted with a train for Elsenham. *H. C. Casserley*

Top right:
On the Wisbech & Upwell Tramway in 1951, 'J70' class tram locomotive No 68225 heads a train of fruit vans. The following year diesel locomotives arrived on the tramway and completely ousted steam in 1953. This was the first such displacement in the country. Ironically the March-Wisbech line retained steam operation until November 1963, the last steam-worked line on the GE section. *LCGB*

Above:
At Saffron Walden on 13 September 1953, an ex-North Eastern Railway 'G5' class 0-4-4T has arrived with a train from Audley End. Like so many country branch line stations, Saffron Walden had only one platform. *D. T. Rowe*

Above:
Like many country junctions, Long Melford is no more. When this photograph of 'C12' No 67367 was taken, it was the junction of the Stour Valley line and the southern branch from Bury St Edmunds. No 67367 has just arrived from Bury in April 1956.
Real Photos (K2864)

Below:
The epitome of the GE section steam suburban train in its later years. 'N7' No 69655 approaches Hackney Downs on a Liverpool Street-Chingford train comprising a pair of quint-arts in August 1955. *Photomatic*

Above:
An 'N7' engaged in what might loosely be described as gardening: weedkilling duties to be precise. The train is operating from St Margarets to Angel Road, the location is Cheshunt and the date is 25 April 1955. The locomotives is No 69683. *LCGB*

Below:
The humble shunter! 'J69' No 68600 on shunting duties at Hertford East on 13 November 1960. *L. Sandler*

Above:
An interior view of Thorpe-le-Soken junction box dating from 6 June 1951, but showing the sort of scene which had remained virtually unchanged for generations. *BR (Eastern)*

Below:
An official view of a very different signalbox, the electric panel box at Liverpool Street on 2 February 1950. *BR (Eastern)*

Above:
A study in signalboxes at Hackney Downs in July 1960. On the left is the old Great Eastern junction box whilst in the foreground is the new British Railways box. *BR (Eastern)*

Right:
Class J15 No 65474, the Huntingdon yard pilot, arrives at the east station after its return freight trip to St Ives on 16 March 1954. *E. H. Sawford*

Below:
Ongar on a wet day in August 1956. 'F6' No 67212 is on the Epping auto-train. Although mainly worked by 2-4-2Ts, other types did occasionally help out on this service. *Real Photos K3175*

Above:
'K3' No 61915 on a down goods near Littlebury in September 1954. This 'K3s' performed a variety of duties on the GE lines, even working the 'Continentals' and the 'Fenman' on occasions. *Real Photos (24899)*

Below:
Class J39 No 64968 heads an up goods near Broxbourne in July 1955. *Real Photos (23925)*

Above right:
The '01s' were Edward Thompson's rebuild of the '04' class. On 19 July 1958, No 63786 emerges from Audley End tunnel with the 12.25pm Whitemoor-Temple Mills goods. *LCGB*

Right:
Just two days after the preceding photograph, War Department 2-8-0 No 90498 brings another southbound goods through the tunnel. One of these locomotives was the LNER's only oilburner of the postwar period and was used on such duties as this. *G. R. Mortimer*

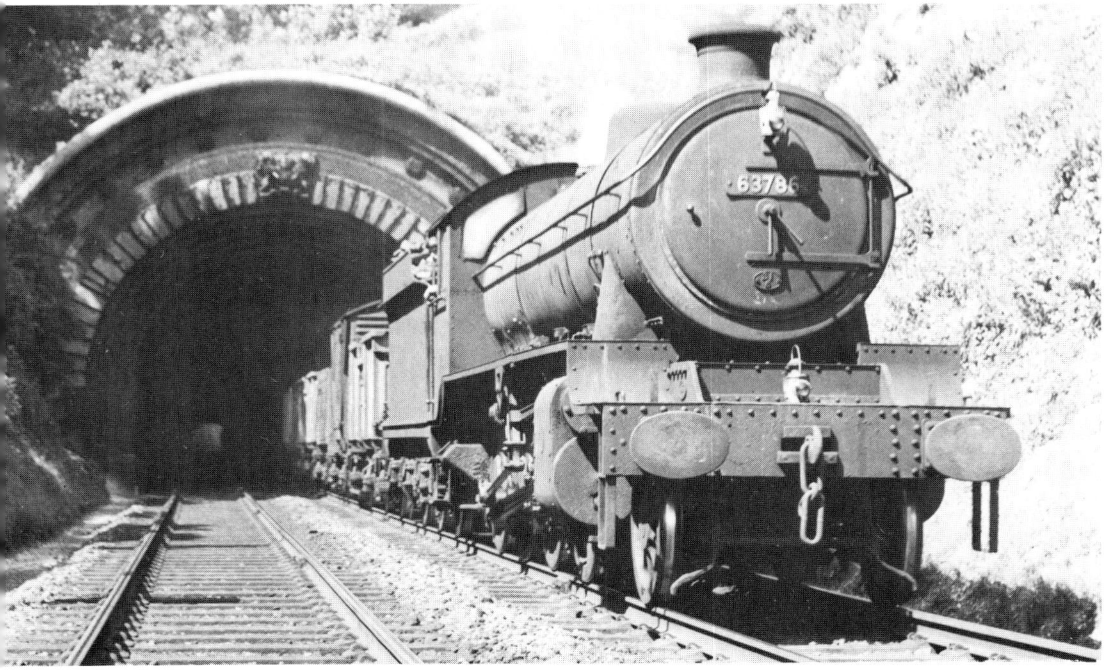
63786

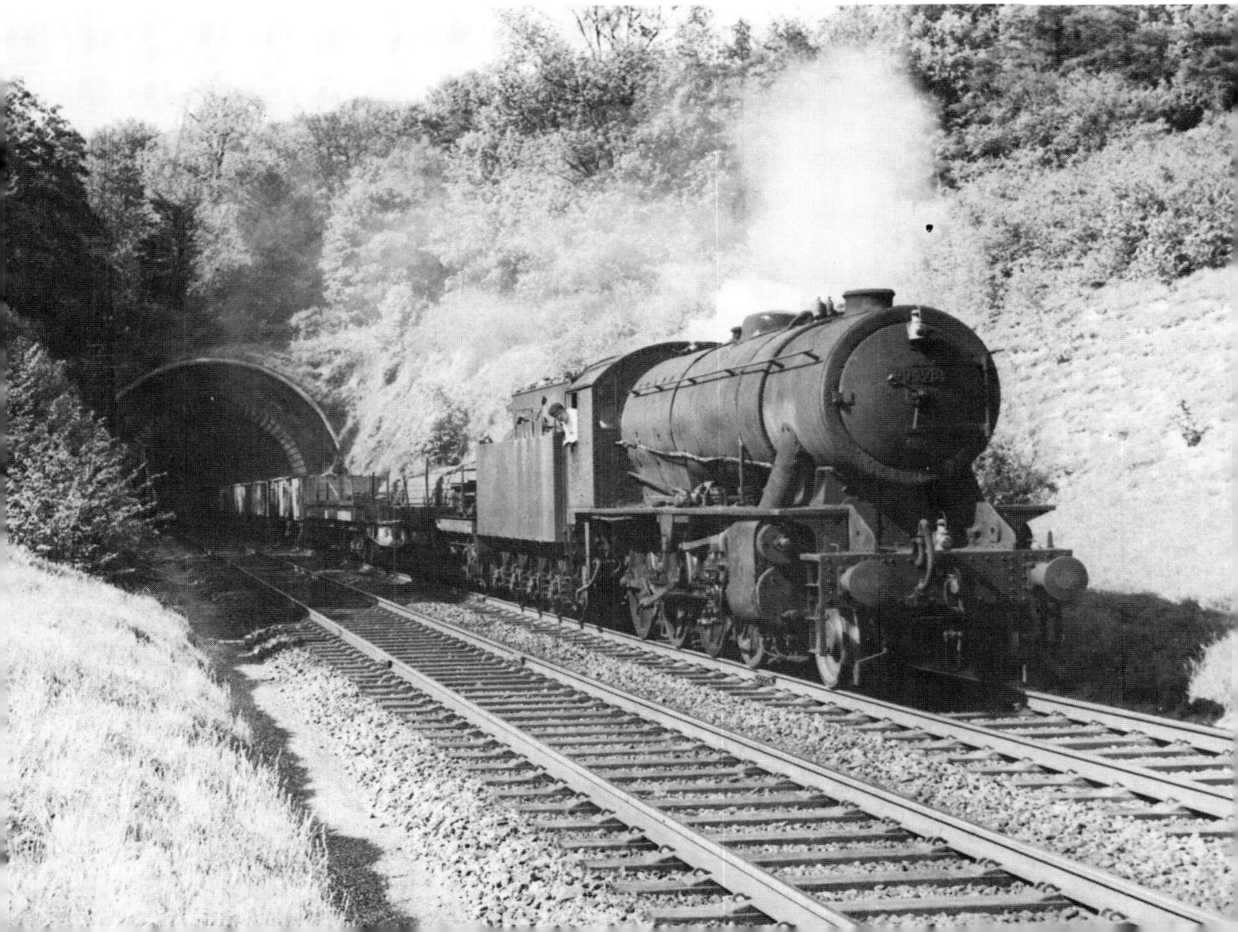

Top:
The necessary duty of ballasting sees 'J17' No 65535 engaged thus at Burnt Mill in December 1955. *Photomatic*

Above:
The 'B1s' were the backbone of the Great Eastern main line passenger services in the later years of steam. In 1959, No 61378 of Parkston shed in seen near Boreham on an up semi-fast.
Real Photos (T5443)

The 'Britannias' though were the pride of the line. Probably the most famous, and the last in BR service was No 70013 *Oliver Cromwell,* **seen here at Ipswich with an up Norwich train. In many ways Ipswich was the hub of the Great Eastern, there being few major places on the section which could not be reached direct from there.** *Oliver Cromwell* **is now preserved at Bressingham.** *Real Photos (T7483)*

A Standard '9F' on the GE section. No 92014 of Stratford passes Cheshunt on 25 April 1955 with a Whitemoor-Temple Mills coal train. Owing to their weight '9Fs' were not allowed to work beyond Stratford. *LCGB*

Above:
At Wickford in 1957, a photograph by Ken Nunn which expresses the modern image of the day on the Great Eastern. In the bay platform a Wickham two-car diesel multiple-unit waits to leave for Southminster whilst on the down line 1,500V dc electric multiple-unit No 21 leads an eight-car train for Southend. *LCGB*

Below:
In 1957 Ongar finally got its tube trains. Although 1935 experimental stock was mainly used in the early days, both 1938 and standard stock also featured on the service. In this view at Ongar on 28 April 1962 a three-car set of standard stock departs for Epping. *L. Sandler*

Above:
In 1957 came the first main line diesels to the Great Eastern lines. At Shenfield Brush Type 2 A1A-A1A No D5504 heads a Liverpool Street-Clacton train on a rather wet day. *P. J. Sharpe*

Below:
The Metropolitan-Cammell DMUs first appeared in 1955 and have been amongst the most successful types of unit on the GE section. On 24 October 1958 a two-car unit on the 1.44pm Swaffham-Thetford calls at Roundham Junction. At this time the station was open for railway staff living nearby.
Hugh Davies

Above:
The five railbuses built by the German company of Waggon und Maschinenbau, and used on the GE section, were intended for use on those lines where the traffic was insufficient to warrant the use of a conventional train. Unfortunately with the exception of the Braintree branch, all the lines on which they were used closed. Railbus No E79960 at Maldon (East) in 1960 is about to depart for Witham. The line, together with the railbus-operated Saffron Walden line, was a victim of the notorious Beeching Report. *L. Sandler*

Below:
Whilst diesel replacements may have arrived for branch line passenger services, steam remained

supreme on goods trains for a little longer. On 24 October 1958, 'J17' No 65561 is on the 12.37pm from Walton at Barnham on the Thetford-Bury St Edmunds line. *Hugh Davies*

Above right:
A new age dawns in East Anglia as English Electric Type 4 diesel-electric No D203, then just a few months old, heads the up 'East Anglian' express near Manningtree on 3 February 1959. *BR (Eastern)*

Right:
A view of the new Harlow Town station taking shape during the electrification of the suburban service on 30 September 1959. *BR (Eastern)*

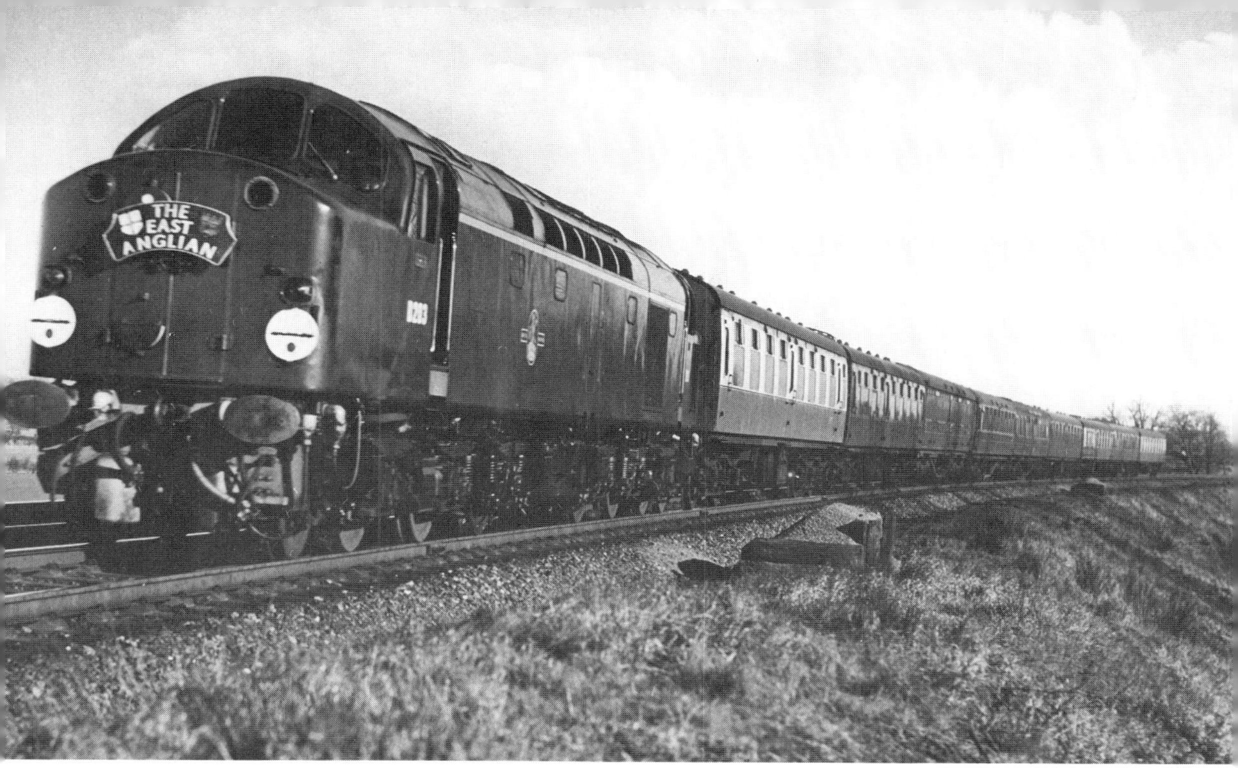
THE EAST ANGLIAN

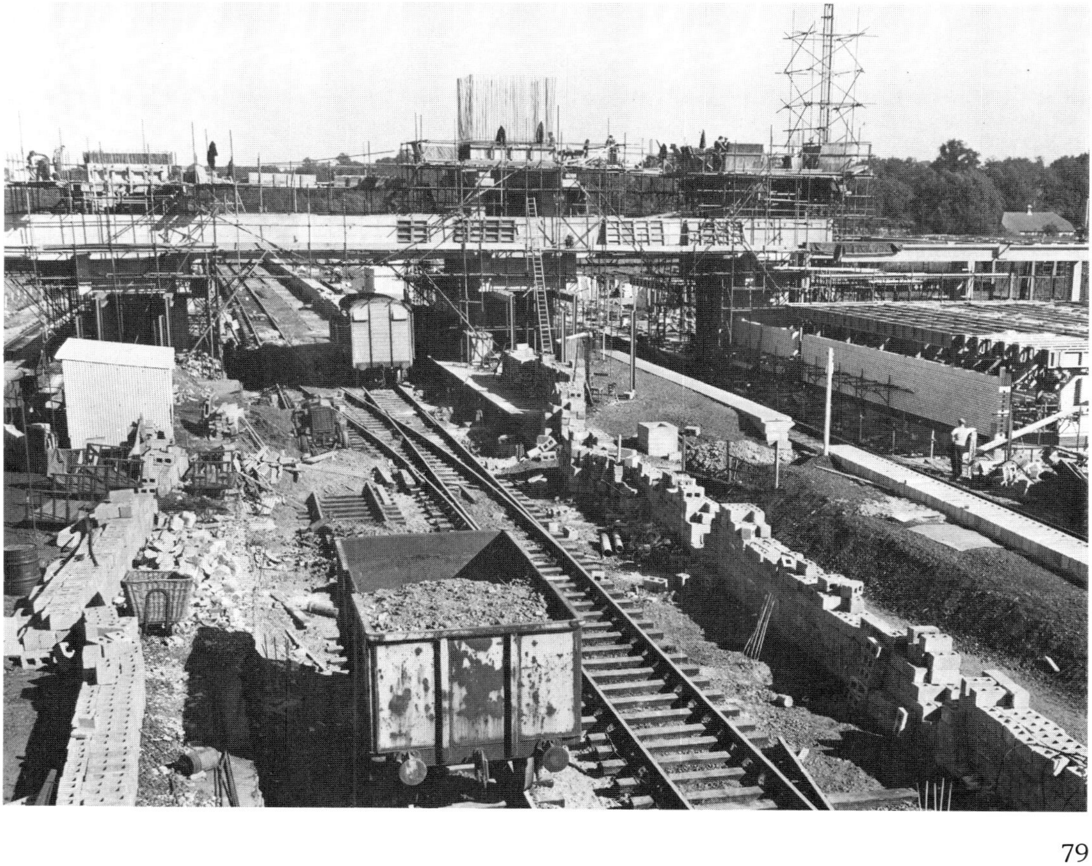

Above:
On Monday 16 March 1959 electric trains using 25kV ac began operating on the Colchester-Clacton and Walton lines. This was the first line electrified by BR on this system. On 30 March of that year, electric Multiple-units Nos 212 and 206 are seen at Colchester forming the 3.56pm train to Clacton. The leading unit's destination blind reads 'St Botolphs'. These were ac versions of the dc units on the Liverpool Street-Southend line. *K. L. Cook*

Below:
For the North East London electrification two types of multiple-unit were delivered. One type was a four-car unit containing first and second class accommodation and the other was a second class only unit. One of the latter, No 404, forms the rear portion of a nine-car Enfield-Liverpool Street train departing from Lower Edmonton. *P. J. Sharpe*

Above:
At the same time, new four-car units were delivered for the East London suburban services. These differed from the North East London units only in terms of the builder of their electifical equipment. No 159 arrives at Wickford on a Southend-Liverpool Street service. *P. J. Sharpe*

Below:
A grimy 'N7' class locomotive No 69725, representing the old order, leaves Liverpool Street with a service to Enfield on a wet 3 November 1960.

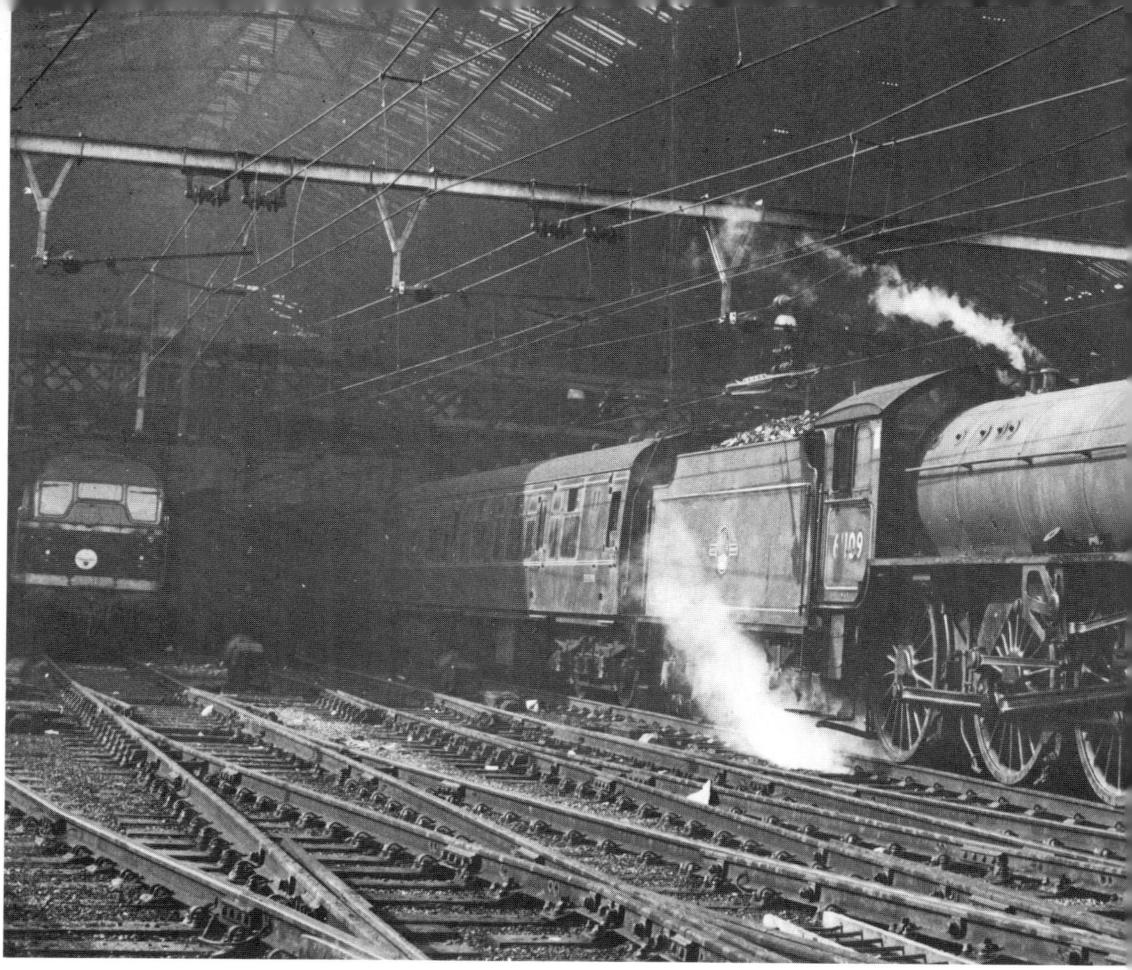

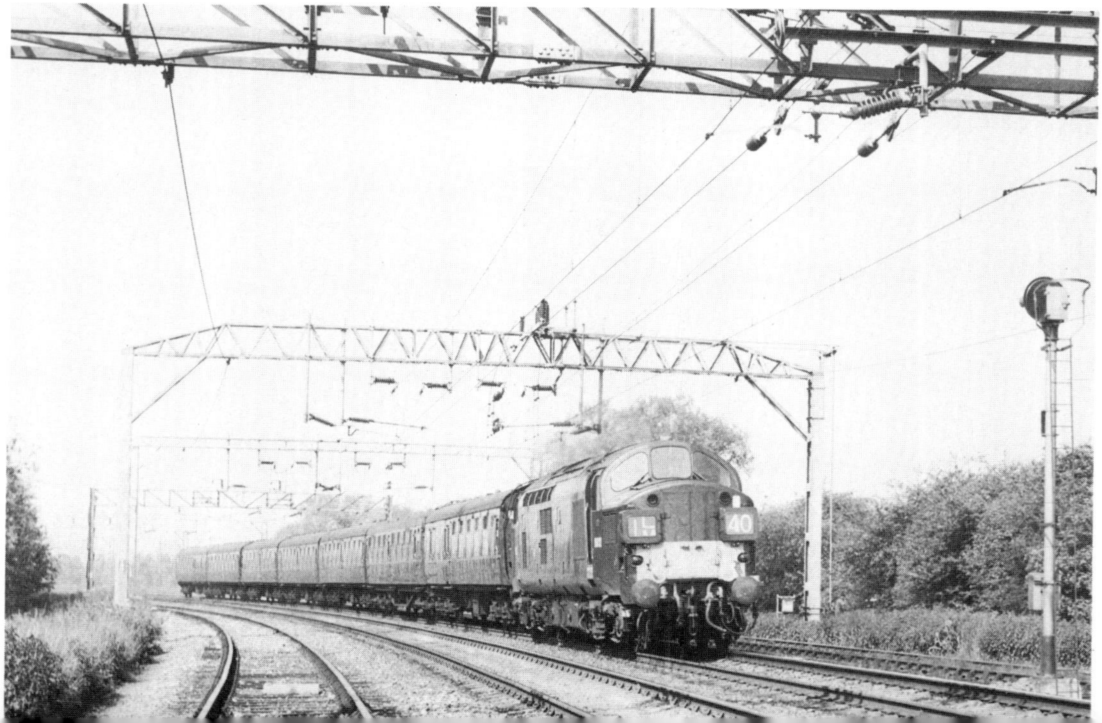
40

Left:
'B1' class 4-6-0 No 61109 is ready to leave Liverpool Street with the 10.30am departure for Norwich on 10 September 1960. *Dennis C. Ovendon*

Bottom left:
The introduction of the English Electric Type 3 diesels finally finished off steam from the Norwich line. They in their turn were displaced after only a few years by the Brush Type 4s on the Norwich line and they took up duties with the Brush Type 2 locomotives on the Cambridge line. On 1 June 1966 No D6722 approaches Roydon with a down morning express. *P. H. Groom*

Below:
The British Thompson-Houston Type 1 Bo-Bo diesels replaced steam on branch line freights from 1959 onwards. On 14 April 1965, No D8226 prepares to leave Hadleigh (Suffolk) for Ipswich. Unfortunately owing to Dr Beeching the line was in its last week of operation. *G. R. Mortimer*

Top:
It is 28 August 1960 and Ivatt Class 4 2-6-0 No 43089 prepares to leave Kings Lynn with the 4.15pm train to March. The Ivatt Class 4 locomotives were used on the Midland & Great Northern lines, and only saw regular services on the Great Eastern after much of the former railway was closed in 1959. No 43089 had, however, been a Cambridge engine in the mid-1950s. *L. Sandler*

Above:
Compared to other lines the end of GE section steam went almost unnoticed. To the Palace Gates-Stratford-North Woolwich service and the Harwich boat trains fell the honour of being Stratford's last steam passenger trains. On the former service anything that could be used did appear. On 3 July 1962 Standard Class 4MT 2-6-4T No 80097 prepares to leave North Woolwich, with another member of the class in the background. No 80097 and several others were used by Stratford during its final steam summer following their displacement by electric trains from the former London, Tilbury & Southend. *H. C. Casserley*

Above right:
Seen from the same position as the previous view is 'L1' class 2-6-4T No 67734 at North Woolwich with a Stratford train in May 1962, with a second 'L1' visible at the rear of the train.
Real Photographs Co (K4996)

Right:
Steam finished at Stratford on 9 September 1962. The Palace Gates-North Woolwich service ceased on 5 January 1963. For the intervening months Brush Type 2 diesels hauled the trains. On the last day of the service No D5619 brings the very final train to Palace Gates into Noel Park and Wood Green. *Martin Beckett*

Above:
In July 1967, a Derby three-car suburban diesel multiple-unit brings a Cheshunt-Liverpool Street Train under the Tottenham and Forest Gate line just after leaving Tottenham Hale. This service was not electrified until May 1969. *P. H. Groom*

Below:
In August 1966 Brush Type 2 diesel No D5573 heads a down Cambridge train just north of Broxbourne Junction. *P. H. Groom*

Above:
On 18 September 1965, British Railways Type 2 Bo-Bo No D5037 of Ipswich eases the 2.02pm Yarmouth (South Town)-Liverpool Street through Halesworth. The locomotive is painted in two tone green livery. *G. R. Mortimer*

Below:
English Electric Type 3 Co-Co No D6705 in standard green livery with yellow warning panels passes Stratford with a parcels train on 10 July 1967. *P. H. Groom*

Above left:
One of the short-lived North British Type 1 single-cab diesels No D8405 enters Temple Mills yards from the North with a transfer freight on 14 June 1967. *P. H. Groom*

Left:
The British Thompson-Houston Type 1 diesels led similarly short lives. On 9 June 1969 No D8200, less than two years from withdrawal heads a Stratford-bound freight at Copperhill Junction. *P. H. Groom*

Top:
On 12 April 1965, British Railways Type 2 No D5045 joins the Framlingham branch at Wickham Market Junction on the daily goods train. *H. N. James*

Above:
A charming view of the ornate station and signalbox at Wolferton, used by the Royal Family for Sandringham, seen in August 1966. *P. Hocquard*

Top:
The Brush Type 4 diesels first appeared on GE lines in 1964 on freights. In August 1966 No D1556 in two tone green heads a down freight north of Broxbourne. *P. H. Groom*

Above:
In 1965 the Brush Type 4s, later Class 47, took over the Norwich passenger services. On 30 April of that year No D1760 passes East Suffolk Junction at Ipswich with the 2.20pm Norwich-Liverpool Street. *G. R. Mortimer*

Above:
The first main line electric unit for the Clacton and Walton services had undergone its test runs on the GE lines in the summer of 1962, but the full electric service did not start until 1963. On 10 July 1967 unit No 622 leads a down train through Stratford. At this time these EMUs were still in their attractive original maroon livery. *P. H. Groom*

Below:
On 23 August 1966 unit No 519, one of the four-car electric multiple-units built for the North East London suburban electrification leads an eight-car Bishops Stortford train just north of Broxbourne.
P. H. Groom

Above:
One of the original ac units, No 219, in British Rail's all over blue livery for suburban and local multiple-units leads an eight-car Bishops Stortford train near Broxbourne in July 1970. *P. H. Groom*

Below:
At Sudbury in November 1965, a Derby lightweight two-car diesel multiple-unit leads a Colchester-Cambridge train into the station. Only the front unit is in use. The rear unit is locked and in transit. *G. R. Mortimer*

Top:
In August 1968 a two-car Metropolitan-Cammell DMU approaches Lowestoft hauling a four-wheel utility van. DMUs are permitted to haul vans so long as the total weight does not exceed the power available. The leading car is still in green livery, whilst the second has already been repainted in BR blue. *P. H. Groom*

Above:
On 2 June 1983 a Cravens two-car DMU stands at Bury St Edmunds having just arrived from Cambridge. *Charles Phillips*

Above:
On 9 October 1974 a North East London three-car EMU climbs Bethnal Green bank on a Chingford train. *G. R. Potter*

Below:
A Clacton/Walton-Liverpool Street service formed of Class 309 units Nos 601 and 604 passes Marks Tey on 19 July 1980. Note the alterations to the windscreen. *Michael J. Collins*

Above:
Workhorse of the GE section. Brush Type 2, now carrying TOPS No 31.263 (originally No D5693) passes Lea Bridge with an up mixed freight in October 1977. *Martin Higginson*

Below:
17 August 1978, Class 08 No 08.661, the first of its class to be allocated to Ipswich, passes Ipswich station with a freightliner trip working from Ipswich yard to Griffin Wharf. *John C. Baker*

Below:
**No 313.034, one of four Great Northern inner
suburban EMUs at that time allocated to Clacton
approaches Colchester with a local train from
Clacton on 5 April 1980.** *Michael J. Collins*

Bottom:
**On 31 May 1983 the North Norfolk Railway's
preserved 'J15' No 7564 stands at Sheringham. At
the time of writing this is the only preserved Great
Eastern locomotive capable of steaming, ironically**
on the former Midland & Great Northern Joint
Railway! The North Norfolk Railway also has 'B12'
No 8572 and two of the German railbuses, as well as
an LMS-designed 0-6-0 diesel shunter formerly
shedded at March. The Stour Valley Railway,
Chappel & Wakes Colne, has the last 'N7', No 999,
whilst 'Y5' 0-4-0ST No 229 is preserved at North
Woolwich. The Nene Valley Railway at
Peterborough has the BR Class 7MT No 70000
Britannia. *Charles Phillips*